CONFIDENT Teens

MASTER COMMUNICATION SKILLS, REDUCE ANXIETY, INCREASE SELF-ESTEEM, AND DEVELOP LASTING RELATIONSHIPS

J.R. CARITAS

Contents

Introduction

Communication is your ticket to success if you pay
attention and learn to do it effectively.
—Theo Gold

There are some things all people fear.

One of them is that nightmare coming true where you show up at school wearing only your underwear, or worse—nothing at all! Everyone is laughing, pointing, and posting pics on Instagram! The height of embarrassment and the end of your life as you know it right then. But there's another fear. Perhaps worse because, unlike the underwear dream, it happens all the time.

Saying the wrong thing at the wrong time to the wrong person!

No matter your age, making a fool of yourself in front of others is social suicide.

It's why Alex chose not to speak unless spoken to, even with his parents. He thought that by keeping his mouth shut and avoiding conversations, he would be safe; safe from public humiliation; safe from becoming the next cyber sensation (for all the wrong reasons!) He dressed down so as not to attract attention. His hair covering his face was a shield, not a style. He wished he could just turn on the magic and have the courage to say what he wanted confidently, but the painful truth was he could never get it right.

Alex was an introvert. Not the natural life of the party. Not a funny guy. He always dreamed he was the guy telling jokes and having all his friends laugh for the right reasons at the right time, but for

Alex, it was an unrealistic wish. He just wasn't made that way. Forget standing in front of the class to give feedback or do an oral presentation. Just speaking with his friends or talking to girls gave him the sweats. To be honest, friends were scarce! It was too painful to try and make new ones.

The words always got choked in his throat as he wondered, "What if I get it wrong?" "What will everyone think of me?" or "What if no one likes me?" What little self-image he had needed to be protected at all costs. He just had to make it through school, and maybe it would one day get better. But he had seen other adults who were reserved, shy, and awkward. He realized he might be safe, but he would be trapped, maybe forever!

Have you ever felt this way before? Ever asked the same questions as Alex? You might be an outgoing person, good at interacting with people, but deep down, you have these same insecurities and worry they might pop out at the wrong time in front of everyone. You may be naturally shy or find it challenging to find the right words. You might want just an extra edge when it comes to speaking to others. Then you're not alone!

Zendaya, the Emmy Award-winning actress, lacked confidence when she was younger. She said, "I was really shy. Like, to the point where my parents went to counselor meetings and stuff, like, how to get them out of their shyness" (Simao, 2020). Ed Sheeran struggled at school to overcome his introversion, and Taylor Swift was never invited out because she was a loner.

The good news is that confidence is not something only a few people have while the rest of us just suffer. It's something every single person can learn and improve. Like any skill, if you have some basic pointers and guidelines, all you need to do is put them into practice, and you too, can communicate with others and be in a group without constantly being afraid of messing up. The good news is this book has all the tools you need. The best news is it's not hard to put these pointers and guidelines into action—right now!

By understanding the obstacles and triggers, you will begin to see where the minefields are, how to dodge them, and not get blown up. Learning these clever tricks will give you the edge Alex was hoping to find. Realizing how to control a situation and not let it take charge of you will mean you don't have to hide any longer. Knowing who you are and how your brain and hormones function are important tools. This book has these answers and more.

I was a bit like Alex. I had insecurities, fears, and doubts. I also had to navigate obstacles and hope I would not implode in humiliation. I still have days where I'm unsure what's about to happen next, and it can be scary, but after many years of putting these techniques into practice, I am much more confident. It is possible for anyone to get better and improve. I know because I have taught and helped thousands of young people like you to get there.

Through my studies and experience in teen ministry, I have gathered a treasure chest of tips and tricks, allowing me to help teens build lasting friendships and see the worth inside of them while inspiring parents to better understand their teenage children. I've been doing this for decades, and everything I know is laid out for you here. You simply need to read on.

Alex came in to ask for my help. The next president or overnight YouTube sensation (for all the right reasons) may not be in his future. That's not in his nature. But now he's confident and happy. He's developed good, solid friendships. His parents witnessed a miraculous change, and their relationship with him has never been better. He's not scared to say what's on his mind. He's not worried he'll be the joke of the day when he opens his mouth. He's not afraid anymore.

But it took some work. Like any skill, it took time. Alex had to practice, and along the way, he discovered he was not alone. He found the world was not against him as he always believed. He discovered people who wanted to help him and had the answers he desperately wanted to know. I walked this road with Alex, just like the one I am willing to walk with you. It will be slightly different because we're all different, but the destination is the same:

A more confident YOU!

ONE
We Are Social

Then the LORD God said, It is not good that the man
should be alone; I will make him a helper fit for him.
—Genesis 2:18 ESV

You're stranded on an island. You can only take one thing with you. What will it be?

It's a revealing question because it shows our interests and what we value in life. Most answers are similar: a book, a knife, matches, chocolate, a toothbrush, a pillow, and so on. While those things might make us more comfortable or keep us alive a bit longer, somewhere along the way, we'll eventually die! Our physical bodies might fight to stay alive until we are rescued, but socially, we will wither and die!

Without a friend, a companion, or a survival buddy, we're toast!

WE NEED OTHERS

Humans are not meant to be alone. We were made and designed to interact, have relationships, to exist with one another. On a deserted island with someone you trust, the odds of survival multiply dramatically. Alone in the wilderness, you have a 20% chance of making it, while in a group, it increases to 80% (Woods, 2022). In the movie *Castaway*, Tom Hanks may have been on his own, but he would not have made it if it weren't for his "friend" Wilson he created. A volleyball with a handprint face was his BFF. He spoke to it, debated with it, and cried when it drifted away. It kept him company and kept him sane.

Survival does not just mean having the sharpest knife; it also means having the right people by your side. Scientists have found living alone or in isolation increases your chances of dying sooner by up to 32% (Holt-Lunstad et al., 2015). To live a happy, healthy life, we need relationships.

We need other people! We are social beings. It's the way God made us. Even though Adam had everything he needed to keep him healthy, strong, and busy, God saw he needed someone to talk to and relate to. It's the same for every one of us. No matter who we are, there's a part of us longing for other people. And it's not just about surviving; it's about being happy. In a Harvard study involving hundreds of participants, those people who spent time with others were much more fulfilled and much happier than the rest (Templeton, 2017).

It's why we have families, communities, and groups bonding us together. Nobody is an island, nor should we ever be stranded alone on one!

IN A GROUP, BUT ALONE

Tiana has a family. Tiana even has a few "friends." There are hundreds of teens in her school, moving around her; rushing to class; playing sports; copying each other's homework; and swapping lunch. But she's still alone like a small boat pushed about amongst the waves. She drifts through the sea of classmates with no one taking notice—a lonely vessel in an ocean of people.

Just because there are others around us doesn't mean we're not lonely! It's a paradox, a contradiction. And it's one of the best places many of us can hide—in plain sight. We smile like Tiana always does in family pics and class photos, but deep down, we're disjointed, cut off from the pack, just like her. And it's not just a few... there are thousands, millions who feel this way.

A survey in 2019 revealed three out of five Americans say they experience this feeling of being lonely; that's 61% (Cigna, 2020). This trend seems to be the same in other countries across the world, with most of those being teens. Whether it's the pressure of making friends or trying to adjust to all the changes at home, school, and in their bodies, those like Tiana find it difficult to make strong enough connections so they don't feel as though they're alone.

The Covid-19 pandemic didn't help this. But it did put a big spotlight on what many are going through and show how more and more young people are feeling disconnected. For months, the world was isolated, with everyone on their own islands trying to survive. The façade of happy families and strong friendships quickly fell away. People were left stranded with nothing but their phones and their TVs. And it doesn't matter how many "friends" you may have on Instagram or social media; without real face-to-face communication, all that's left is a few good pictures and the gnawing feeling of being alone on this planet.

TALKING IS GETTING HARDER

What's the big deal about talking? Parents are constantly nagging about communication when it's clear you're already engaged in hundreds of conversations. Your thumbs move at such vicious speeds across your phone the screen sends a warning of overheating! You're a wizard at sending just the right GIF, the perfect emoji to say how you're feeling. Isn't that what they want? Communication?

Face-to-face meetings have been overtaken by texting and calling. Since the smartphone entered our lives, catching up with friends has become so much easier. Even our language has shortened, so it's quicker. LOL! Instead of finding all the right words to tell someone you can't or you're too busy, you simply swipe right or left, and it's no longer a problem. The hard work of building and nurturing relationships has become instant. Communication has dropped from our faces to our thumbs!

Research has found teens in the 12–17 age group choose digital conversations rather than actually meeting up with a friend (Pew Research Center, 2010). The shift over the past 30 years has moved us further away from hands-on, in-person, eye-to-eye contact. We're far more connected but way more removed! Another paradox.

In Jamal's home, everyone has a phone. They need them for safety, staying in comms with each other, keeping reminders, and knowing what's going on. But his parents noticed a change. He became narrow-minded and inward-looking, even though he was always chatting with others on his phone. Popular in his social network, he was constantly replying and sending texts. At dinner, Jamal was distracted, always waiting for a text to be answered and listening for new notifications.

His link to the world had become an addiction. And just like any other bad habit, it has side effects. Brad Huddleston says, "the more we stimulate the brain, over time it starts to shut down, and we start to lose emotional feeling" (2021). Technology is wired to tap into our brains, releasing dopamine when we hear a message come through or receive digital stimulation. Dopamine is a natural, feel-good hormone we get when we experience something enjoyable, but it doesn't last very long at all. It makes us feel good for a very short moment, leaving us anxious for the next dose.

That's not the only drawback to greater digital communication. Speaking and interacting face to face suffer, so real interactions, bringing lasting pleasure and satisfaction, diminish. Teens like Jamal develop communication problems; they can no longer read body language correctly; there's no discernment; they struggle to listen; and eye contact is non-existent. Jamal has the gift of being able to ignore everyone in his house, especially when he's deep into an important text. But you can't swipe left for everything you don't want to deal with at the moment.

At a stage when he should be learning and adapting skills to help him develop throughout the rest of his life, Jamal is bent over his screen. It's not that phones and computers are bad; we need them to navigate our way through this social network that has become life. But if we don't want to end up like Jamal, we'll have to find some healthy ways to make it work for us and not the other way around.

Remember, we're social animals made to interact with other people. Communication and relationships play an essential role in our lives regardless of whether we like them. Whether it's friends, family members, or peers, as long as they're in our lives, we need to connect with them on a deeper level than just a social media post! We can't let screens replace real people; otherwise, we're back to living on an island, even with our profile getting multiple likes, comments, and followers.

Like Alex, Tiana, and Jamal, there's another step to take to get us out of our social quarantine and back to dry land where we can begin building genuine and meaningful connections. And if you're more of an aggressive communicator or a very outspoken individual, there are still many areas we can work on, so others can better enjoy your company. It all starts with learning better communication skills which means listening as well as talking.

If we don't want to be trapped on a social island, then learning a few methods of communicating with real people and making good friends is the way forward.

EXERCISE

Do you talk a lot, or do you talk more through instant messages, chat, and text? Are you quiet and reserved, or somewhere in the middle? Can others hear you coming from a mile away, or do they even notice you're around? We're all different, and the way we communicate may not be the same as the next person.

Here's a fun exercise to get us started. There are no right or wrong answers. It's just to see what kind of person you are, whether you talk a lot, message a lot, or neither! For each question, choose the letter that most sounds like you.

Questions

1. When was the last time you verbally spoke to someone?
   a. A few minutes to an hour ago.
   b. It's been several hours or more than a day.
   c. Earlier today.
   d. A few hours ago.

2. Roughly how many texts/instant messages do you send per week?
   a. a lot
   b. under 40
   c. over 250
   d. over 100

3. Do you ever talk to yourself?
   a. All the time.
   b. Never.
   c. Hardly ever.
   d. Sometimes.

4. What's your social life like?
   a. I'm always around friends.
   b. It's average.
   c. I spend only my weekends with friends.
   d. It's healthy.

5. Has anyone ever told you that you talk too much?
   a. Yes, more than a few times...
   b. No.
   c. Yes, once or twice.
   d. Yes, but I think they misjudged me.

6. Are you more extroverted (outgoing) or introverted (reserved)?
   a. I'm definitely extroverted.
   b. I'm about as reserved as it gets.
   c. I'm more on the outgoing side, but I have some introverted tendencies.
   d. I'd say I'm equally balanced.

7. When was the last time you engaged in conversation with a stranger?
   a. Today.
   b. I never talk to strangers.
   c. Within the last two weeks.
   d. Within the last month.

8. Do you ever get in trouble for talking out of turn or not raising your hand?
   a. Yes, I'm always getting into trouble for little things like that.
   b. No.
   c. Maybe once.
   d. It's happened a few times.

9. Do you like public speaking?
   a. I love it!
   b. Hate it with a passion!
   c. It doesn't affect me either way.
   d. It's not my first choice, but I can do it when necessary.

10. Do you ever talk or make comments during a movie or TV show?
    a. Yes, I can't help myself.
    b. No, and I can't stand it when other people do.
    c. Only if it's an outstanding show.
    d. I yell at the TV when watching sports games.

11. How often do you talk on the phone?
    a. Two or more times per day.
    b. Once a month or less.
    c. Maybe once a day or every couple of days.
    d. Once every few days to a week.

12. Are you on Twitter?
    a. Yes, it's my favorite social media platform.
    b. No.
    c. Yes, but I only use it occasionally.
    d. Yes, but I prefer other sites.

13. Is it easy to make new friends?
    a. I can befriend almost anyone.
    b. No, it's pretty difficult.
    c. It's usually easy, but other times it's a challenge, depending on the situation.
    d. I already have all the friends I need.

14. What is one word your friends would use to describe you?
    a. unpredictable
    b. quiet
    c. interesting
    d. complex

15. Do you ever interrupt your friends while they're talking?
    a. Yes, but they know how I am.
    b. Not usually.
    c. Yes, but I'm working on not doing it so much.
    d. It depends on what we're talking about.

Which letter did you choose most often overall? If you answered mostly:

a—You talk a lot. You love talking! It's one of your many strong suits. Conversing with lots of people is what keeps you going, and you always have lots to talk and laugh about. You enjoy being the life of the party and the center of attention!

b—You definitely don't talk too much. If anything, you don't talk enough. You're a quiet person who enjoys listening and observing more than talking. You prefer time by yourself rather than going to large parties.

c—It's unclear whether you talk too much, but there's a strong possibility that you do. You probably talk more than you listen, but you try your best to give others more than enough time to get their say. Others enjoy your company if they can get a word in as well.

d—You talk an average, healthy amount. You try not to dominate the conversation, and you go out of your way to encourage others to talk while you listen. But some situations and environments cause you to talk more than you usually would, like when you're nervous or under stress.

(Bri O., 2017)

TWO
Confident Listening

If one gives an answer before he hears, it is his folly and shame.
—Proverbs 18:13 ESV

Motormouth. Chatterbox. Babbler. Verbal Diarrhea. We all know someone who talks too much. They just go on and on and on and on... It might even be you! Just because a person can speak doesn't mean they're a good communicator. As with everything, there are two sides to making it work properly. Listening is crucial, maybe even more important than being able to say what you want. Without it, it's just one-way traffic—someone who dominates the conversation—a yapper.

Shy people like Alex are often good at listening because that's all they do. But for Bella, she just had so much to say and all the words to do so. Her marks for class presentations were through the roof. Every chat with her friends was a chance for her to express herself and let them know her opinions. That's what her parents had taught her: believe in yourself and don't be shy. But her friends often rolled their eyes when Bella's mouth opened—she could talk, and that was it. Bella hardly ever listened or let others have a chance to speak.

So, what exactly is listening? The International Listening Association defines it like this: "Listening is the process of receiving, constructing meaning from, and responding to spoken and/or non-verbal messages" (2011). It's not just opening your ears to hear the words but also understanding them before replying. That's the key right there—*knowing* what the other person is honestly saying.

We think hearing and listening mean the same thing, but that's where our first mistake occurs. Hearing is what happens when sounds enter your ear. Unless you have hearing problems, you'll hear your mom telling you to clean your room, the next-door dog barking in the middle of the night, and your teacher droning on about some boring historical person who's been dead too long to be remembered!

Listening is quite different. It requires focus and a little extra effort. You might hear the story, but you have to pay attention to how it is told, the language used, the voice and tone of the speaker, and their body language. It's far more than just words. Bella never picked up when her friends were bored with yet another lecture on finding the right boyfriend. She missed those little tell-tale signs and responses indicating it was time for her to shut her mouth.

We have two ears and one mouth,
so we may listen twice as much as we speak. —Epictetus

WHY IS LISTENING IMPORTANT?

There are several advantages to using your ears to listen and your mind to digest what is actually being said. By actively listening, you will find you can begin building the platform for open, solid, lifelong relationships with incredible benefits.

- **More Trust**

  Who wants friends they can't trust? Nobody! Trust is the cornerstone of any relationship. By trying to listen, it shows your interest in your friends and what they're saying. It's not something you can fake. Others can tell if you're really paying attention. Nodding your head while scrolling through your latest tweets as someone is talking to you shows them you're not interested. When you mumble "Uh-huh" every so often, it doesn't mean you're genuinely engaged in the conversation.

But when you listen with your ears and your mind, it makes the other person more comfortable. This makes them more open to sharing and establishes trust. They will be more open with their thoughts and feelings.

- **Fewer Misunderstandings**

When your parent asks if you've finished your homework, and you reply, "I'm done with homework!" It could mean you completed it or you just quit. No more doing homework for you ever again! It's all in the way it's said. One student heard the teacher say their project was to be an essay on "Youth in Asia." He spent two hours researching and writing on it, only to discover it was supposed to be on "Euthanasia!" Miscommunication can be funny, but it can also end in disaster. One of the best ways to burn a friendship is to half-listen.

Misunderstandings usually happen because we don't listen to each other properly. It's not hard to mishear or misinterpret what others are saying, especially with our ears constantly plugged into wireless headphones! But listening to the context, and understanding the reasons behind what was said, will often help us steer clear of an embarrassing mistake.

- **Less Conflict**

  "Nobody ever listens to me!" When we feel as though we have not been properly heard, we can become angry and frustrated, leading to shouting, tears, and resentment. We want to feel respected, heard, and understood, but this won't happen if no one listens to us. It doesn't mean they have to agree with everything we say. We're all different, so we'll have different opinions or views on things at times. However, when others listen to our unique ideas, we can avoid arguments and discuss without raising voices and tension.

- **More Empathy**

  Other people's shoes might be smaller, bigger, more stinky than yours, or a brand that doesn't suit our style. Being able to "step into those shoes," see things from their point of view, and feel some of what they're going through, it's not easy. We all have different assumptions and biases because of the way we were brought up. It's easy to give in to the temptation of focusing on what we think and know instead of what the other person's going through.

  By truly listening, it becomes easier for us to understand better where others are coming from. You will not only know what they're saying but also what they're feeling. This deeper understanding improves your empathy and is an incredible building tool for healthy, lasting, and meaningful relationships.

- **Better Friendships**

  Shallow friends are the worst; they'll ditch and run the moment things get too tough or too serious. No one wants people like that in their lives. The only way to have deep friendships is to listen more. There is a direct link between good, solid companions and an increase in physical and mental health (Soken-Huberty, 2021). Taking the time to listen will bring all the benefits already mentioned and lay a foundation for long-lasting relationships.

Faithful friends are a sturdy shelter: whoever finds one has found a treasure. Faithful friends are beyond price; no amount can balance their worth. Faithful friends are life-saving medicine; and those who fear the Lord will find them. Those who fear the Lord direct their friendship aright, for as they are, so are their neighbors also. —Sirach 6:14–17 NRSVCE

- **Better Productivity**

You know the person in class who asks the teacher a question about something they just answered? Groan. If only they listened a bit more, then they'd get it the first time like the rest. There's always one in every class—it might even be you! Good listeners are able to understand things faster, avoiding raising their hands to ask dumb questions. They're also really good at group projects and team tasks. Just because you're talking a lot doesn't mean you're contributing; listening is sometimes the more effective course of action.

- **Better Leadership**

Look at the top sports teams and see the types of coaches or captains they have. Notice it's not someone who shouts orders for all the players to obey. One of the most innovative entrepreneurs and businessmen, Richard Branson, said, "If you want to stand out as a leader, a good place to begin is by listening" (Zipkin, 2014). Anyone can become a good leader if they work on improving their leadership skills, and that means using their ears and minds. When you're actively listening, it becomes easier to understand what others are saying. You are not only developing respect from those around you, but you're also forming a better picture of who they are and how you can lead them. The best teams have someone who listens to what others say and values everyone's opinions.

STYLES OF LISTENING

As we've seen, sometimes closing your mouth can be the key to excellent communication. It has many benefits that become building blocks to better relationships. But listening goes even deeper than just opening your ears and your mind. There are different types of listening, and mastering these will strengthen your ability to be a confident person when it comes to communicating.

- **Discriminative Listening**

  You may not remember much as a baby, but you came into this world with particular skills. One of these was discriminative listening. Without knowing what our parents were blabbering about over our cribs, we had some kind of idea of what they might be saying. By not focusing on the words, instead listening to the voice, changes in pitch, tone, and other verbal cues, we knew we were in trouble for drooling all over dad's precious TV remote. We were able to identify when things were good by picking up on the cheerful sounds that came from the adults crowding around us, pinching our cheeks, and patting our heads. The specific information was not necessary. We just knew who was talking and if it would be a happy moment.

But it's not just babies that can do this. Watch a foreign-language movie without subtitles, and you'll quickly know when the bad guy has entered the scene or two people are falling in love. Discriminative listening skills allow us to analyze the speaker's tone, so we can understand their feelings or make sense of what they are saying. Even non-verbal cues can be used to figure out what's being said. The speaker's body language and facial expressions will give you massive clues.

Think about how it works in your own life. You want to go somewhere with your best friend, and you tell them about your ideas for the evening. Even though they agree, their body language shows something is wrong. The way they uncomfortably shift in their seat or struggle to make eye contact can be giveaways that perhaps your plan hasn't got a thumbs-up reaction. Discriminative listening skills give you these tell-tale signs. Hopefully, you pick up on the clues and ask what's wrong before the night is completely ruined!

- **Comprehensive Listening**

  Comprehensive listening is developed when you're a child. From that cute baby who could only gurgle and pick up voice tones and other cues, you begin to focus on the words being said. It's all about understanding the meaning of the message by using your knowledge and vocabulary.

  It adds to discriminative listening; instead of just looking at the clues given through voice and body, you listen to what's being said and form a much better picture of what is happening. It's an active form of listening because it requires you to participate in some way.

In a lecture or class, you have to pay attention and take notes to understand better and retain the information being given. Watching a documentary or news report requires you to be alert to the words being said. This is comprehensive listening.

- **Empathic Listening**

  Emotions drive this listening style. Instead of just focusing on what the other person is saying through their words, you concentrate on their emotions or feelings. This is handy when you want to offer support. Instead of just listening to what they say, you begin to understand their feelings.

  If one of your friends is stressed because of family difficulties, then by utilizing empathetic listening, you will understand what they're feeling and the reasons behind their anxiety. Instead of saying you're sorry for them, you get a better insight into their situation, allowing you to offer the support they need.

  You see pain with your eyes, but you sympathize with your ears. Sometimes the greatest way to serve someone is just by listening. Behind every need is a story. —Rick Warren

- **Analytical Listening**

  This type of listening is excellent when you need to analyze complex information. By using critical thinking, you don't just accept what's being said; you figure out what's a fact, what's fiction, whether you agree, and what to do with the information. It's crucial for problem-solving and deciding how to handle a complex situation. It works best when you look at the bigger picture and then compare it with everything you already know.

A judge or someone watching a debate will use this approach to decide the outcome. Music producers and songwriters use this listening style to figure out which notes, chords, words, or harmonies to add or discard for the perfect finished song or melody.

- **Selective Listening**

    This is a typical form of listening we all employ at some time. It's best known as selective hearing or listening to only what we want to hear! Most of us use this listening style to fall asleep when trains pass by or airplanes land and take off around our homes. You might use it when mom asks you to do a chore you've ignored for a while. You don't even hear your own name. Instead, you only listen to what you want to hear because that's what meets your needs at that moment.

    It's not all bad. Because it's selective, it means you can be totally absorbed in whatever you have chosen to listen to at that moment: your favorite song or an engaging conversation with a friend. You show how much you appreciate what you have heard by giving positive responses.

ACTIVE LISTENING

The most basic and powerful way to connect to another person is to listen. Just listen. Perhaps the most important thing we ever give each other is our attention. —Dr. Rachel Naomi Remen

Conflict and misunderstanding followed Ethan like a stray dog. There were always arguments about everything and nothing, whether it was his friends at school or his family at home. Sometimes he would barely say a few words out loud before the arguing started all over again. Like a yapping, angry hound, there were always too many words yelled in frustration. Ethan blamed others for not understanding him!

It took a few years before Ethan realized the problem wasn't them; it was his inability to listen properly. With some help, he recognized he was reacting like a dog, always looking for a fight! Once he realized he just had to listen first to get others to listen to him, his relationships began improving. The stray dog disappeared!

Ethan learned that with active listening, you must entirely focus on what's said instead of simply hearing the words. When you listen, it's not just your ears that you engage, but all your other senses become involved. You not only understand the words spoken but the overall message conveyed in the voice, body language, and even the eyes.

But there's more. Using these same actions, you can show other people how you're really listening—not just with your ears, but your face and body and carefully chosen words. Verbal and non-verbal listening methods will open a whole new world for you, just like they did for Ethan.

Non-Verbal Active-Listening Skills

A simple nod of the head means yes, and it shows you agree with what's being said. If you frown, then the other person might suspect you have a problem with what they're saying. By using these five simple techniques, you can become a better listener. And as we already read, there are so many benefits for those who listen!

- **Smile**

A smile brightens up your face and sends a positive message. It doesn't have to be big and cheesy. Even a small, quick one shows you're listening. Try to make it genuine because a fake grin is annoying. A genuine smile touches your eyes.

It also increases your cool factor! A psychology study found that people who smile are perceived to be much more relaxed than people who don't. It also keeps you calm as your brain produces chemicals that tell you, "I'm enjoying this!" (Boone, 2022)

If it's not a natural thing for you to do, then practice in front of the mirror. Make sure your smile is big enough to activate the muscles in your cheeks and those around your eyes. This is a truly genuine smile.

Another way to inspire confidence is by smiling. A simple smile can be a doorway for many opportunities. It suggests that you are accommodating, willing to listen, and friendly. —Mick McPherson

- **Eye Contact**

Looking around when someone is talking to you or refusing to make any eye contact shows a lack of interest in the person speaking. When you look into the other person's eyes, mutual gazing is very gratifying. Please don't do it too long or hard! They might think you're *too* interested or a little angry. Just the right amount of eye contact sends the message: I'm interested and listening.

And you also benefit because, with just 30% eye contact, you remember more of what is being said (Van Edwards, 2021).

Again, use a mirror to practice. Don't forget to glance away every so often as you do so it's not an uncomfortable stare.

- **Posture**

Are you tired of hearing your parent telling you to sit up straight, not slouch, and put your shoulders back? They are not all wrong!

Your posture shows a lot about what you think or feel in a situation. If you sit slumped, it shows you're not fully engaged. Attentive listeners usually lean slightly toward the speaker to show interest in what's being said. Remember to be respectful of the speaker's personal space when you do this.

Hold a straight, open, and comfortable position as you listen. Keep your arms and legs uncrossed, as it shows you're not tense or closed off to the speaker. Crossing arms and legs is defensive and can indicate you don't really want to listen to the other person.

Again, you benefit from this open posture as people who sit with folded arms remember 38% less of what's said (Van Edwards, 2021).

- **Mirroring**

This technique effectively shows that you feel the same way or share something in common with the speaker. Notice what the other person does and mimic it (not how your little brother or sister does when they're trying to annoy or irritate you!). If it's a slight nod of the head, how they sit, or hand gestures, do the same.

It helps us cooperate and even persuade others to our point of view (Van Edwards, 2021). Please make sure these gestures are subtle; otherwise, they can be seen as mocking.

- **Limited Distraction**

    If you want to show you're listening, the best thing to do is limit all distractions. Loud music, blaring TVs, running game consoles, crowded coffee shops, and lots of fidgeting all show you're not fully engaged. It doesn't mean you need to sit like a statue in a monastery, be natural and genuine.

    And whatever you do, don't phub! You might be so used to scrolling through your phone that you do it without thinking while someone is speaking. This is phubbing—ignoring or snubbing someone by being busy on your phone (Holland, 2018)!

Verbal Active-Listening Skills

Teaching Ethan a few of these skills changed his conversations from war-zone battles to laughter and enjoyment. He had to practice, but soon they became even more natural. He nodded, sat up straighter, and even mirrored his parents' hand gestures. It worked. But we also worked on a few things Ethan could say to show he was listening in a conversation, which made a huge difference.

The words you respond with show if you're actively listening. If the teacher hands out an assignment and asks if everyone understands, then a good question can show you are actively listening. Here are three techniques you can learn to become a better active listener:

- **Positive Reinforcement**

  Everybody likes to feel they have done or said something right! This trick works wonders. But be cautious and don't overuse these. Simple positive reinforcement phrases are: "Please go on," "Tell me more," "I understand," and "That sounds interesting." Even the word "Really?" does wonders.

- **Attentive Silence**

  Even fools are thought wise if they keep silent, and discerning if they hold their tongues. —Proverbs 17:28 NIV

  Silence is golden… so shut your mouth and get rich! You don't always have to speak or make a movement to show you're listening. Sometimes being quiet will do an even better job. Attentive silence is a verbal, active-listening skill meaning to hold your tongue when someone else's talking.

  Remember Bella? She never stopped talking. She made the horrible mistake of not waiting until her friends had finished before she blurted out what was on her mind. By interrupting, Bella showed she wasn't listening. As the verse says, even a fool can look like they're wise if they just close their mouth long enough to listen.

- **Open-Ended Questions**

  This is a clever way to show you're listening. Ask about what's being said. The easiest way is to turn what the other person just said into a question: "So, you're saying that you don't sleep well because you're worried about your parents?" It doesn't have to be the perfect question, and you don't want to do this too often, or it can become both irritating and annoying.

Practice this at home. When your mother wants you to do something, clarify what she's saying by asking, "You want me to take the trash out?" Just make sure you don't do it too often. She might think you're being disrespectful!

In Ethan's case, the arguments didn't completely stop. Dealing with different people, personalities, and circumstances means you can't just apply one formula and think it will work every time. But for the most part, he and his parents were less stressed as he took the time to listen. He had to bite his tongue many times. He had to swallow the argument building in his throat. He had to really try hard not to see everything from just his own point of view.

Ethan's mom and dad silently thanked God for the peace that came back into their home. His group of friends enjoyed his company, knowing there wasn't always tension when they hung out together. His teachers even noticed a difference. All by applying a few easy tips and tricks he learned.

EXERCISE

See whether you're an active listener by completing this easy exercise:

While someone is talking, I...	Usually	Sometimes	Rarely
Plan how I'm going to respond.	1	3	5
Keep eye contact with the speaker.	5	3	1
Take notes as appropriate.	5	3	1
Notice the feeling behind the words.	5	3	1
Find myself thinking about other things while the person is talking.	1	3	5
Face the person who is talking.	5	3	1
Watch for significant body language (expressions, gestures).	5	3	1
Interrupt the speaker to make a point.	1	3	5
I am distracted by other demands on my time.	1	3	5
Listen to the message without immediately judging or evaluating it.	5	3	1
Ask questions to get more information and encourage the speaker to continue.	5	3	1

Repeat in my own words what I've just heard to ensure understanding.	5	3	1

Scoring:

44–60: You're an active listener.

28–43: You're a good listener with room for improvement.

12–27: You'll need to focus on improving your listening skills.

(AT&T, 1995)

Listening is about being present, not just about being quiet. —Krista Tippett

THREE
Communication Styles

*Don't use foul or abusive language. Let everything
you say be good and helpful, so that your words will
be an encouragement to those who hear them.*
—Ephesians 4:29 NLT

Bella talks as though she has a train to catch (or maybe she's holding on while the train is pulling her along a track of words!) Everything tumbles out so fast, many of the words automatically join to create new combinations and new words. Her arms and hands fly around as she talks, making sure everyone in the group hears her story of what happened yesterday.

On the other hand, Alex might as well be working for the postal service. Any message could take forever to be delivered at the speed he talks. Slow, hesitant, each sentence like pouring syrup. He prefers to hang back; not speak, if possible; not look anyone in the eye; and simply blend in if there's a group.

We all have different ways of expressing ourselves, but our choice of words is what becomes important. Written, text, or spoken, these are all forms of verbal communication. The right words send the intended message. The wrong ones can cause confusion and chaos!

Bella and Alex actually went to the same kindergarten growing up, and they had the same teacher. Day in and day out, they stared at the same flashcards and repeated the exact phrases as they learned words and sentences. But there's more at play when it comes to how we get our unique styles of communicating. Much of it has to do with how we are raised and the friends we hang out with; they all rub off on us and determine how we do things, act, and speak. And then there's also the fact that we're all uniquely different.

We each have different communication styles, depending on who we are and the mannerisms we have picked up along the way or been taught at school and home. Quiet, loud, reserved, stuttering, hesitant, forceful... the way we talk and convey our ideas defines who we are. It's how we participate in conversations with our parents, teachers, and friends.

EXERCISE

Try this exercise to understand better the type of communication style you use most. Read through the questions and only check the ones that are most applicable to you. Leave the others blank. Remember to be honest with yourself as you go through these.

Section 1

☐ Do you try to push your feelings away rather than express them to others?

☐ Do you worry expressing yourself will cause others to be angry with you or not like you?

☐ Do you often say things like "I don't care" or "It doesn't matter to me" when you do care, or it does really matter to you?

☐ Do you keep quiet or try not to rock the boat because you don't want to upset others?

☐ Do you often go along with others' opinions because you don't want to be different?

Section 2

☐ Are you most concerned with getting your own way regardless of how it impacts others?

☐ Do you often yell, talk loudly, or swear when you speak?

☐ Do your friends worry about saying the wrong things to you?

☐ Do you like taking the lead in conversations?

☐ Do you have an attitude of "my way or the highway"? Have you ever heard anyone describe you this way?

Section 3

> ☐ Are you often sarcastic when you feel angry?
>
> ☐ Do you give people the silent treatment when you're angry with them?
>
> ☐ Do you say one thing but think another, going along with another person's wishes even though you want to do something else?
>
> ☐ Are you reluctant to voice your emotions, but you express them in other ways, like slamming doors or other aggressive behavior?
>
> ☐ Do you worry that expressing yourself will make others angry with you or stop liking you, so you try to get your message across in more subtle ways?

Section 4

> ☐ Do you believe you have a right to express your opinions and emotions?
>
> ☐ When you're having a disagreement with someone, are you able to express your opinions and emotions clearly and honestly?
>
> ☐ When communicating with others, do you treat them with respect while also respecting yourself?
>
> ☐ Do you listen closely to what others are saying, sending the message that you're trying to understand their perspective?
>
> ☐ Do you try to negotiate with others if you have different goals rather than being focused on getting your own needs met?

(Van Dijk, 2012)

Now, look at where most of your check marks are located.

If the majority are in section 1, then it appears you're using more of a **passive** communication style when interacting with others.

If most of your checks are in section 2, you could be using a more **aggressive** approach in your conversations.

If they're in section 3, you might be employing a **passive-aggressive** manner when communicating.

Finally, finding more checks in section 4 means the communication style you could be using most often when you engage with others is an **assertive** one.

You could even think of these as four quadrants where you might be mostly one type with a little bit of another mixed in.

Each communication style has good qualities on its own. However, three of these styles can become damaging to long-term social interactions by pushing people away, causing mistrust, or hurting and damaging friendships.

Let's look at the three that can become unhealthy and a fourth that uses the best qualities of the other three to form a healthy way of communicating and producing lasting relationships.

AGGRESSIVE COMMUNICATION

This is the most obvious to see. The lion that roars. It's a vocal and expressive style, not just the voice but the hands and body language too. This type of communication often dominates or controls by criticizing, blaming, threatening, or intimidating (Warner, 2021). Intense eye contact is used to push ideas across and position the person speaking in control. As a result, these people are not good listeners, giving out commands, and asking loud, abrupt questions.

A group leader may use this style to command respect and get ideas across clearly. But if there's no balance in how they use it, they will just come across as loud and rude. If you want to be respected, you need to respect others. Similarly, if you want others to listen, you will also need to listen to them. Aggressive communicators often forget this and can leave those listening feeling controlled and underappreciated.

You'll recognize aggressive communicators by phrases like:

- "You're wrong. I'm right!"
- "We're doing it this way!"
- "It's all your fault!"

Add in some finger-pointing, crossed arms, and eye-rolling, and you have an aggressive speaker. To be on the receiving end of this can be very hard to take, making friendships challenging to build with anyone using this style all the time.

PASSIVE COMMUNICATION

If we have our four quadrants with each style in a block, then this one will be on the opposite side of aggressive, not a lion, but a timid mouse. Instead of being open and vocal, making sure their ideas and plans are heard and carried out, these people draw back. They will go with whatever decision is made even if they disagree with it as long as there's no confrontation! Their feelings or needs are not expressed, and they let others walk over them (Warner, 2021).

Passive communicators tend to listen more than they speak which might seem reasonable, except not conveying what you're thinking, feeling, or want can lead to misunderstanding or resentment.

Most people who use this style do so to avoid conflicts at all costs. They don't mind being different from others as long as it means not stepping on toes. But nobody wants to be a doormat or have one as a reliable friend. Just going with the flow doesn't help anybody in the end. It may be good in a few circumstances, but using this way of communicating all the time will not create the space necessary to develop deep friendships.

These are common phrases used by passive speakers:

- "I'm fine with whatever."
- "As long as it keeps the peace."
- "It really doesn't matter."

Unlike the aggressive lion, these mice can't make eye contact at all and use their hair, clothing, arms, and legs to hide themselves.

PASSIVE-AGGRESSIVE COMMUNICATION

Squashed between these two is passive-aggressive communication. The fox! They might look like they're just mice, being passive, not rocking the boat, and keeping quiet, but the way they act out is subtle and sneaky (Warner, 2021). They bottle up their resentment inside and then find ways to let it out, often causing sabotage or hurt.

They don't like confrontation but will mumble and mutter, which can cause division in a group through gossip. Because they don't want to be outspoken and acknowledge their emotions, they struggle to convey what they're feeling. They might seem okay with something, but their actions tell the opposite.

They can say things like:

- "It's okay with me, but don't be shocked if it upsets someone else."
- "Sure, let's do it your way (then mutters a nasty comment under their breath)."

Just like a fox, they use the silent treatment to great effect and send strong messages of what they really feel through their body language.

ASSERTIVE COMMUNICATION

There's a fourth quadrant where the person speaking can say how they feel without dominating or controlling others like a lion. Unlike the fox, they can also listen without simply hiding away like the mouse and use body language to match their words. Assertive communication is where you can say what you feel and want while considering the feelings of others. This is the owl.

By being honest without disrespecting others, they communicate their feelings and thoughts on a situation. Often people can misinterpret them as aggressive because they're confident in themselves and not scared to say what they feel (Warner, 2021). But their way of involving others and ensuring they're also involved and heard makes them different.

Here's a scenario involving all four styles when brought the wrong meal at a restaurant (Warner, 2021):

Passive: "It looks great, thank you."

Aggressive:	"Are you dumb? This order is not what I want! Take it back and sort it out!"
Passive-aggressive:	(mutters first) "It looks great if you like the wrong food, ha ha!"
Assertive:	"Thanks, but this doesn't look like my order. Can you correct it, please?"

Fortunately, if you discover you have a particular style of communication, it's not set in concrete. By using these techniques and practicing, you can move from being stuck in the aggressive corner toward the assertive one. Or you can learn to become a bit more vocal and confident which will move you from hiding in the passive quarter.

Knowing your communication style definitely helps. If you're honest with yourself, can look in the mirror, see the real you, and admit where you might be making mistakes, then you're on the right track. This will allow you to see any gaps you need to focus on to improve.

Like Alex, you can work on stepping out and voicing your opinions more. Like Bella, you can tone down the volume and speed, allowing room for others. We all need some help to become better versions of who we are.

Great speakers you wish to be like, were products of mistakes. Mistakes shaped their speaking skills. If you're afraid of making mistakes, you will remain there for so long! —Israelmore Ayivor

FOUR

Healthy Communication Techniques

*Everyone should be quick to listen, slow to
speak, and slow to become angry.*
—James 1:19 NIV

We may be natural speakers, our mouths filled with words like Bella,
who can say more in a day than most people get out in a whole
week! Or we're too quick to speak our minds and make our point
the way Ethan does. We might be a bit more reluctant, like Alex or
Tiana, preferring the "less is more" approach. But whichever way,
we don't get it all right every time. Every one of us can do with some
clever methods to enhance our speaking and improve body language
during conversations.

Learning techniques can help you engage better with friends and
strangers. Not only will you become a better speaker and listener,
but others will notice a maturity and confidence in you that wasn't
there before. In this chapter, we will look at several healthy habits
to practice enhancing how we speak to others.

VERBAL SKILLS

What we say is obviously a key part of any conversation. Our words have the power to connect, heal, or destroy. Too often, we don't give our words enough credit for what they can do to another person or a situation. We say things cheaply, but they can end up becoming expensive when we're dealing with their consequences.

Words are free. It's how you use them that may cost you.
—KushandWizdom

Here are some healthy tips to assist you, whether you're talking to friends, family members, teachers, coaches, neighbors, or anyone else.

- **Listen First**

    As we've already seen in Chapter 2, listening is often more important than speaking. There's nothing worse than seeing the other person about to jump in with what they have to say before you've even made your comment. One way to improve communication is to listen to what's being said.

    It makes the other person feel their contribution is valuable and important to you. They want to engage because they can see you're taking them seriously, even in a casual conversation. Giving others room to speak and taking note of their words is one of the most critical aspects of communication. It's like a golden rule!

    It is hard to listen when you are talking, or
    when you are thinking of a response!
    —Catherine Pulsifer

- **Think Before Responding**

This might sound like a silly technique, but it's one we forget the most: Think before you speak! You don't have to rush in and fill the silence gap. Pause! Reflect on what has just been said. Formulate your answer. Others will respect you more because what you say carries more value than something you just rambled off.

This is also very helpful for texting! Don't push send before you've thought about your reply and read it again. You may be surprised by how often a mistyped or autocorrected word can send the wrong message.

- **Express How You Feel**

You know best how you feel and what you think, so focus on that first. Don't presume to know what the other person is feeling—that can be dangerous! They can say it's not true, deny it, and start an argument. No one can dispute your feelings because that's you! Don't try and convince others about your feelings, as someone else might consider that response as you being aggressive. Simply stating your feelings without raising your voice can set the tone for a good conversation.

This doesn't mean the conversation must revolve around you, what you think, and how you feel. Give everyone room to express their thoughts and feelings, being extra careful not to tell others how you think they should feel.

- **Focus on "I"**

  Stay away from phrases that include "You should…" or "You must…" These can be heard as condescending, demanding, or lead others to feel you're speaking down to them. Stay away from telling others what you think they *should* do. Stick to speaking from your own point of view using "I" instead of "you." Trauma therapist, Kaitlin, advises using this formula sentence: "I feel _____ when _____. I need _____." (Klipsch-Abudu, 2020).

  Instead, it's a way to keep from telling others what they must, should, or can say. We're not experts on anything, even though we might think we are. We're all learning, and others will feel more inclined to share with us if we take this approach.

- **Keep It Down**

  During a conversation, argument, or debate over something, it's easy to get defensive or passionate and raise your voice. But it doesn't help in a social interaction. Even if you're just excited, your voice can ramp up a couple of notches and become a distraction. When you feel the volume rising, take a breath. It's okay to take a step back before things storm out of control.

  It's also important to include others who might have soft voices, giving them the opportunity to express themselves and drawing them naturally into the conversation. If you're naturally loud, keep checking your volume every few minutes during a chat, argument, or presentation.

  *Raise your words, not your voice. It is rain that
  grows flowers, not thunder. —Rumi*

• **Say Sorry**

Elton John wrote the song "Sorry Seems To Be the Hardest Word," capturing both the meaning and difficulty of saying out loud the word sorry. It's always hard to say sorry, but apologizing goes a long way to smooth out a conversation that has gone the wrong way. We all make mistakes and saying the wrong thing can get you into heaps of trouble if you don't admit your error. "Sorry" (and meaning it) is a magic word for fixing many situations. It also does wonders for your reputation as an honest, trustworthy friend.

This doesn't mean being a pushover or apologizing for everything. You're entitled to your feelings and points of view, and expressing them is very healthy and shows confidence. Someone who is always saying "Sorry!" can be irritating and seen as less genuine after a while. Use this technique only when you know you've stepped over the line or made someone else feel unworthy of being in the conversation.

EXERCISE

Have some fun and see if you can sort these different types of communication into their two correct groups. Circle those most resembling verbal communications, and underline those most resembling non-verbal communications.

Instagram	FaceTime	Waving	Face-to-face Chat
Shouting	Braille	Singing	Phone
Dancing	Whispering	Diary	Facial Expressions
Emojis	Road Signs	Texting	Voicemail
Storytelling	Laughter	GIF	Group Video Gaming

Answers:

Verbal: FaceTime, Face-to-face Chat, Shouting, Singing, Phone, Whispering, Voicemail, Storytelling, Group Video Gaming

Non-verbal: Instagram, Waving, Braille, Dancing, Diary, Facial Expressions, Emojis, Road Signs, Texting, Laughter, GIF

NON-VERBAL TECHNIQUES

Not all communication is in our words. Without counting the words, about 55% of what's said is actually done through body language and 38% through the voice (UT, 2020). That means most of what's said is not spoken! If that's true, then we need to take more notice of the entire other person and not just the words spoken.

We've already seen a few examples of how we can listen better by the way we sit, look, and move. These are critical, not just for listening but also for what we want to say to the other person. The message we're sending can be strengthened by what we do. It can also make a point without saying a word.

Let's look at a few healthy tips you can learn for your face, body, and voice.

- **Read Body Language**

    You can learn a lot about a situation or a person before they even open their mouths if you're observant. Watching gestures, facial expressions, and eyes can tell you if a person is confident, uncomfortable, or even lying! Spotting these will help you communicate better. It's a bit like being a detective.

    What would you say about Alex, who wore his hoodie the whole day, even when it was hot? Just a fashion statement or a desire to be left alone and stay *hidden*? What about Tiana, the lonely girl, biting her nails while waiting for someone? Just working on her manicure or nervous? And let's think about the person in a group who keeps looking at you without saying anything. Hmmm…

A simple eyebrow flash can send a message faster than words, and studies have shown it's used around the world as a way to greet other people (Van Edwards, 2021). Only lasting a fraction of a second, this gesture of quickly raising the eyebrows shows you know someone, are about to make contact, or are interested in the other person. A similar message can be sent by a slight lift of the chin toward another person you want to acknowledge. This chin-up movement, often used by guys, is a simple, quick, and effective non-verbal greeting or acknowledgment.

It's not hard to pick up these small details; it just takes a little bit of practice. Try this short two-minute exercise with another person.

Sit facing each other with your knees almost touching. Assign one person the role of speaker and the other the role of listener.

Round One: The speaking partner sits on their hands to answer a personal question for 60 seconds. The listening partner must not speak at all, but only listen and observe the words and actions of the speaking partner. *Ask the speaking partner to describe the scariest ride they ever rode or the most frightening situation they have ever experienced.* The listening partner pays special attention to any body movements the speaking partner makes as they answer the question.

Round Two: Swap the roles of the speaking and listening partners and repeat the exercise asking the new speaking partner to *describe the first time they danced in public or had to speak in front of a large group.*

Evaluate: After finishing the exercise, review with each other any body movements you observed as your partner answered their question. These can be as subtle as rocking back and forth, movement of the arms, squints in the face, nods of the head, closed eyes, head bobbing, shifting of shoulders, and leg movements. Be as thorough as possible with anything you observe as a listening partner. All these are ways the speaking partner communicates with you in addition to their words.

• **Straighten Up**

Alex naturally slouched. Every time he sat, he slumped, and when he stood, he was always leaning against something as though he needed help staying up! It sent all the wrong vibes. He looked like he was trying to withdraw, hide or slide away from the conversation.

Sitting up with your head focused on the person speaking shows you want to hear and be a part of what they are sharing. It shows confidence. Even if you're walking or standing, the same technique can be used to project a positive attitude. You don't have to be a statue, but by pulling your shoulders back slightly, it tilts your head up, creating a more confident posture.

• **Eye Contact**

We have already seen how important this is in being an active listener but being able to pick up how much or how little a person makes eye contact can tell you a lot. You may have heard the phrase, "The eyes are the windows to the soul," and this is so true when someone is speaking, you can read their secrets (Anon, 2009).

Mutual gazing shows an open, truthful personality, but shifty eyes that look away often or try to stare you down can show when someone is lying (Anon, 2009). On the other hand, wide eyes and large pupils show interest—maybe in what you're saying, or maybe even in you! Then again, someone who keeps gazing around everywhere without focusing on the speaker is nowhere in the conversation.

By simply increasing your gaze on the other person, you can strengthen the bond in your conversation. Just make sure you look away occasionally; otherwise, you will make them feel uncomfortable.

- **Eye Position**

  This concept begins by observing the level of your eyes to the others. Not just how much you look at someone, or they look at you, but the height or depth it's done from can send a message. Usually, your teacher will have you seated while they stand and present the lesson. This eye position commands authority, especially when information needs to be delivered without interruption. You'll find parents take this stance when they're giving *the* lecture about your studies, your room, your hygiene, or your choice of friends.

  When your eyes are on the same level, it creates an atmosphere of inclusion, and everyone's contributions are viewed as equal in the conversation. It's not about a person's height but rather the level of everyone's eyes in a conversation. Watch for people who talk down to you or even prefer to duck their heads and speak up to you. These are messages. Try this simple exercise.

Stand next to someone who is taller than you or someone shorter than you. Notice the level of your eyes next to theirs. The taller person's eyes will be above yours, and the shorter person's eyes will be below yours. Any conversation in this situation could be uneven, with the taller person looking down or the shorter person looking up at you. Now, have everyone sit on the floor, and suddenly all eyes are nearly the same height. So, if you want an inclusive sharing experience, sit down in chairs almost the same height.

- **Personal Space**

Ever felt uncomfortable when someone is speaking just because of how close they are to you? Or too far away? We all have a personal space bubble, and when someone comes in and pops it, we feel threatened or put off. When someone sits out of range of the conversation, it's hard to chat.

Personal space differs for each person. Some people have a no-go zone with landmines and barbed wire around them, which doesn't help. Others want to get close and personal until you can smell the ketchup they had on their hamburger for lunch! It also depends on if you're with someone close to you or with a stranger.

Remember to respect the other person's space but be close enough to engage with them.

- **Clear Voice**

It's not always what you say; it's *how* you say it. How fast or slow you talk, your tone, and the inflection of your voice sends messages to those listening.

Tiana had to learn to open her mouth a bit more so she didn't mumble or slur words. Instead of looking disinterested or half asleep, her friends felt she was more engaged and made sense. She also learned to put more emphasis on her words to stop them from becoming a dull monotone. Suddenly, others listened because what she was saying sounded more appealing.

Ethan swallowed half his words in his attempt to get everything in before the other person could reply. He had to slow down and pronounce what he was saying. Not only that, but Ethan also found swapping a sarcastic or angry tone for a more pleasant one made all the difference. Suddenly, his "Good morning" sounded inviting rather than like he was looking for a fight!

With some help and practice, Alex began using eye contact, sitting up straighter, and expressing himself a bit more rather than simply accepting whatever anyone else said. He still speaks quite slowly, but his confidence towards joining in conversations means he's not just a hanger-on but is now an active part of his friendship group.

Bella has been trying to put the brakes on. She doesn't always get it right, but instead of steamrolling her ideas and stories, she has softened her gaze, not talked down to others with her eyes, and found ways to open the conversation with her friends. Since she started using these simple techniques, there has been much more laughter and sharing.

EXERCISE

Try this True or False Quiz about Non-Verbal Language:

Questions

1. A handshake is body language. **T   F**
2. Positive body language is contagious. **T   F**
3. Just looking will tell you the true meaning behind body language. **T   F**
4. Body language means the same things in different parts of the world. **T   F**
5. Appearance can play a significant role in non-verbal communication. **T   F**
6. Your tone is verbal communication because it involves voice. **T   F**
7. Verbal and non-verbal communication both use all five senses. **T   F**

Answers

1-T   The way you hold the other person's hand tells you a lot about them, whether it's firm and controlling or limp and half-hearted.

2-T   Others feed off a positive approach, and it can change the atmosphere of a conversation.

3-F   You cannot tell just by looking. You have to learn what each movement and gesture means. It takes practice and an observant eye to see and *feel* what's being conveyed.

4-F In Asian countries, looking directly into a person's eyes can be disrespectful, while in India, nodding your head up and down means "No!"

5-T The way you dress says a lot about you. Sloppy, baggy clothes don't show confidence.

6-T The way you say something is significant. A tense voice can convey a message of anger just as much as a soft, hesitant one can display fear or anxiety.

7-F Words only use sound, but non-verbal communication can involve seeing, hearing, smelling, tasting, and touching in different scenarios.

Practicing and using these techniques when you speak to others puts you in a position where you're in control of who you are and what you want to say. This is a good step in mastering communication skills and becoming more confident. Reading into another person's approach to a conversation will give you an extra edge in understanding the entire message as it's being conveyed to you.

Just make sure you don't become a detective, overanalyzing every single movement and change in tone as a sign. Somebody twitching their nose or wiping their eye every so often might not be nervous or lying but actually just coping with an allergy! Instead, give yourself room to see the whole picture, give the other person the benefit of the doubt, and don't assume too much too soon. Blake Eastman of the Nonverbal Group says, "There's [often] a behavioral disconnect between what people want to show and how they show it" (2021).

Coming into a conversation with suspicions or preconceived attitudes will not help you to read body language clues clearly. Have an open mind. Try not to let your emotions dictate what is going on, especially in a serious or difficult discussion. Here's a verse that will help you to have the right attitude in any conversation.

Finally, brothers and sisters, whatever is true, whatever is noble, whatever is right, whatever is pure, whatever is lovely, whatever is admirable—if anything is excellent or praiseworthy—think about such things.
—Philippians 4:8 NIV

FIVE
Avoiding Roadblocks

Words are from the lips; actions are from the heart.
—Rashida Costa

Actions speak louder than words! It's true. Albert Mehrabian researched body language and found about 90% of what we communicate is not through the words we say. Only 7% is the actual words, and the rest is all in the *way* it's said (2020).

That means we can sometimes send messages without knowing it. We can tell others we don't really want to talk to them even though we're "smiling" at them! We can put up roadblocks or obstacles to block discussions just through our facial expressions, the way we sit, move, or even our voices.

The shy teenager Alex used to shut down conversations before they began. Others could see he didn't want to talk, so they hardly ever involved him. Tiana always felt lonely even though there were people around her. She made it clear through both her body language and words that she wanted to remain by herself. She didn't even realize she was advertising it to everyone. And Jamal's addiction to his phone made it impossible for others to engage with him, creating a roadblock to any meaningful chats.

Bella and Ethan aren't shy to speak and actively look for conversation. Still, both of them were making it clear through subliminal actions and words they wanted to be in control, dominate, and make their point clear, leaving little room for any open dialogue.

Anything can become an obstacle to communication creating a roadblock. If we're under stress, have an issue with someone, or react in a certain way, we can put a stop to the way the conversation is going, sometimes without even knowing we're doing it. Roadblocks or obstacles show we're not really listening to or caring for the other people in the social interaction.

VERBAL ROADBLOCKS

> *Kind words can be short and easy to speak,*
> *but their echoes are truly endless.*
> —Mother Teresa

Choosing the right words or the way to say them is crucial to any conversation. The wrong words can end a conversation before it's started. We need to be aware of how we respond to others, ensuring we're not cutting them off and trying to push through our own agenda.

Depending on our words, we can send a message of how we're judging our friends, trying to force a solution on them, or diverting the discussion. Let's look at seven common ways people cause conversations to hit a speed bump and derail.

- **Ordering**

  Ordering is best left to food deliveries, not conversations. Being told what to do or say in a conversation is not what we want to hear. Even if the other person means well, it can put them above us, changing the dynamics of the conversation. No one starts a chat because they want to be ordered around; that's for teachers, doctors, and army captains! As soon as someone starts giving advice by telling us what and how to do it, we feel we want to withdraw or retaliate.

Often, we use ordering without knowing because we want to jump in and fix a problem or situation as we see it. But it's not our job to tell everyone else what they should be doing and how they should do it. We're not experts (even though we might feel as if we are!) Ordering or commanding means we have authority over the other person, and we know better.

Examples of this roadblock often have the following phrases in the sentences:

- "You should…"
- "You have to…"
- "You better…"
- "You will…"
- "You can't do that…"
- "Don't get involved in that…"

Ethan was placed in charge of his team to finish a school project. It didn't go well. He thought by telling everyone what to do; they would know their place and get their job done. This might seem like an efficient method to get the job done; however, it doesn't give the others any room to express their opinions, feelings, or ideas. In the end, the other team members felt they were being treated like children and rebelled, doing nothing. Ethan couldn't understand why they were all so unhappy, making him mad! The school project was a disaster and never got finished!

In conversations, it can be the same. We're always handing out advice, telling our friends how, what, and when. One of Bella's friends told her someone had posted a picture on Instagram that she didn't want others to see. Bella launched into action, telling her she must confront that person, she must tell them to remove the photo, she must not trust... she must... she must... In Bella's call to action, she never listened to her friend before launching her action plan. Perhaps her friend first wanted to share how she was feeling and the hurt she felt because of what was done rather than do anything about it at that moment.

We might have good intentions but giving out orders makes consideration and collaboration very difficult.

- **Warning**

You know when your mom tells you what's going to happen if you're not off your phone and at the dinner table in the next five minutes? That's what this roadblock is like. It's a threat about what's going to happen next. It often involves some kind of punishment if something doesn't happen. The use of a warning is not the way to have open communication.

There's no acceptance of how the other person might feel or any empathy for their situation. When we warn someone of the negative consequences of not doing something, we can offend them. They can become defensive and resent us, just like how we feel when mom tells us to get off the phone! They might reply with "So, what?" or "How do you know?"

Here are some phrases often used when warning:

  ○ "If you don't do this now..."
  ○ "You're asking for trouble if..."

○ "Stop that, or I'll…"

○ "If you do that again, then I'll…"

○ "You'd better listen or…"

Tiana got irritated with her friend. There had been an issue where the other girl received a bad grade for her assignment and was afraid to show it to her parents. She went on and on about it until Tiana had enough. Instead of sympathizing with her friend or helping her through this challenging situation, Tiana threatened her friend to stop talking about it or else she would tell her parents. Their real friendship rested on this ultimatum.

Again, teachers, coaches, and parents use this method a lot to get us to act quickly. In some circumstances, it's necessary. But in a social conversation, it can be a huge roadblock. Most times, we don't even really mean it. We say things to try and get a quick response, but by adding a warning consequence, we put pressure on the other person to obey. The use of warnings in conversations can destroy a healthy relationship.

• **Moralizing**

This roadblock often uses the word "should" in sentences. It's not as harsh as ordering others around or threatening them to do things, but it's just as harmful to communication. These are more subtle in our speech. We use a list of our morals to dictate whether our friends have fulfilled our expectations.

Morals are the invisible guidelines we use to determine wrong from right. But when we use our morals to condemn someone else for what they should or shouldn't do, they can interpret them as judgments against them personally as either good or bad. When the judgment is bad, we stop the conversation by making the other person feel inadequate or unworthy because they're not living up to our standards. They may immediately feel sorry they ever told us anything.

It's another form of criticism. By showing the other person hasn't done what we usually expect of everyone, they're made to feel inferior, not as wise as the person telling them what they should or shouldn't do. It creates anxiety and shame, and instead of being honest and open, the other person will put on a front and pretend for the rest of the conversation.

Some of the tell-tale phrases used in moralizing are:

- "You should've..."
- "You gotta..."
- "It's your responsibility to..."
- "I really think you should..."
- "The right thing to do is..."

Alex's friend was sitting on a bench after school. They both looked depressed, although Alex always seemed that way. His friend told Alex he got a bad grade on a project. Instead of using patience and listening to his friend vent his frustration or offering encouragement, he said, "Maybe you should have spent more time studying instead of playing that video game!" Alex meant well, but he blew it, and they both continued sitting in silence.

We think we're offering helpful advice, but we're actually showing the other person where the standard is and how far they are from it.

- **Criticizing**

We all know what criticism is, yet we use it so often in communication without realizing we're throwing down obstacles for others to engage with us. Nobody likes to be judged. Nobody wants to be blamed. But when we slip these sharp criticisms into our responses in a conversation, that's exactly what we're doing. It's even worse when we do it in front of other people.

Think about when the teacher singles you out for something you did wrong during class. You immediately wish you could vanish, disappear, or be anywhere else. You also feel resentment and hostility toward the teacher, especially if they're right! We'll do anything to preserve our self-image. It's the same when we criticize our friends. They learn it's not safe to share their problems with you, and any chance of open communication shuts down immediately. They may even lash back with criticism just to save themselves from being labeled as a failure.

Very few people like to hang around with critical friends because they're always on the firing line for something that might be wrong.

Here are examples of the phrases critical people use:

- ○ "You're not thinking clearly…"
- ○ "You've got no one to blame but yourself…"
- ○ "I couldn't disagree more…"
- ○ "It's terrible of you to do that…"

Bella critically shot her mouth off at her friend because she heard what her friend had done and was embarrassed. Bella through words like "How could you…?" and "That wasn't right of you…" Bella made it clear how she felt about the situation. Her friend may have been wrong, and Bella may have been right not to agree with the behavior, but it wasn't handled well. The other girl sucked in her lips, dipped her head, and swallowed. She had been judged, and there wasn't much else to share, not even her side of the story!

There's no growth when we're criticized or corrected harshly. Trust goes out the window, and feelings of shame and resentment take their place. There will always be times when we disagree, and it's not always easy to keep our own feelings about something in check, but for healthy communication, a kind word can save us from killing conversations and friendships.

Some people make cutting remarks, but the
words of the wise bring healing.
—Proverbs 12:18 NLT

- **Labeling**

Telling someone what they are or what they're like isn't always the best way forward in a conversation. Labels stick and can be truly hard to ignore once everyone knows about them. We may even say these to our friends, trying to make a joke, but it can backfire when it threatens their self-image. Ridiculing or name-calling is a way of shaming others or humiliating them by labeling them as a certain kind of person. And one thing teens hate is to be put in a box they don't want to be in!

Instead of being a joke or a way of expressing your own view, this can end up irritating those involved. They can become very defensive and fire back with "No, I'm not…" These labels cause them to feel judged, robbing them of who they are and lumping them into a category. It doesn't even have to be a bad label to generate this effect, as good labels such as "team player" or "overachiever" can also produce the same demoralizing impact on a teen's self-image.

Besides actually calling someone a "do-gooder," "lazy," or "diva," we can squeeze labels into sentences like this:

- "That was really *stupid* of you."
- "That was a *nerdy* thing to say?"
- "Your clothes are *trashy*."
- "You *weirdos* always think…"
- "Okay, Miss *know-it-all*."
- "You're acting like a *spaz*."

Jamal chose to text his friend some encouragement when he heard he didn't get picked for the football team. In his text, he jokingly used the word "loser." When he didn't get a reply, he thought maybe his joke was not taken the way he intended. It took a lot of awkward texts and sorry emojis to try and get back on track. Jamal could have avoided the entire situation by not using any labels, which are better on foods than people, and instead taking a few minutes to call and give his friend the encouragement his friend deserved.

Bella made a similar mistake when the girls she was with talked about the neighborhood where they lived. She said, "All you girls who live there always…" immediately drawing a line between her and them. After that, an invisible line separated the group making it difficult to carry on a casual conversation.

Instead of seeing each person for their unique characteristics and abilities, labels cause us to only see them with the traits associated with a particular group.

Do not judge others, and you will not be judged.
—Matthew 7:1 NLT

- **Praising**

You might be wondering why this is on the list of roadblocks. Shouldn't praise be a good thing that can build up and encourage others in a conversation? Yes, it is and can be used this way effectively. However, it also can block communication from being open and honest when done incorrectly or with the wrong intentions.

When we praise someone as a person instead of for their actions, we put pressure on who they are as a person, not what they have done. In a research experiment, school kids were given a standard IQ test. The first group was told they did well because *they were smart* after receiving their results. However, the second group was told they did well *because of their hard work*. When both groups were asked if they wanted to do a more challenging test, the first group didn't want to participate, whereas almost all of the second group were very keen to continue (Sheely, 2014).

If you praise someone to flatter them, or use it too often, instead of building them up, it can backfire. People can read into your attempts at honoring them as not being genuine, especially when it doesn't fit their self-image, or you use it to try to get them to do what you want.

To flatter friends is to lay a trap for their feet.
—Proverbs 29:5 NLT

Here are ways praise is misused:

- ○ "You're so clever. You can help me with…"
- ○ "I couldn't agree with you more…"
- ○ "You're the funniest…"
- ○ "That's what I would do…"
- ○ "Nobody's as fast as you…"

Ethan was learning not to be so argumentative and had been trying a few techniques to improve his communication. He fell into the trap of trying to make the other person feel better by heaping compliments on them. Obviously, it didn't work out as well as he anticipated. His friends grew suspicious of all his flattery. Ethan was trying too hard, and all his words seemed forced and unnatural. Fortunately, his friends realized what he was trying to do, so the damage wasn't so bad that he couldn't fix it.

Don't stop praising people after you've read this because you're afraid you'll get it wrong. When you mean it, praise is affirming and helpful, especially when your praise focuses on the deed, like the great work they performed, instead of on the individual, like you're a great person. Authentic praise is life-giving and deeply appreciated by everyone. Never stop or fear providing it to those around you.

Here are examples of how authentic praise sounds:

- ○ "I like the way *you* did that…"
- ○ "*Your* attitude during… was amazing…"
- ○ "That's very kind of *you*…"
- ○ "I like *your* style…"

- **Avoiding**

Have you ever walked into a store, theater, or mall and glanced up only to see the one person from school you just didn't want to bump into? What do you do? Hide, change direction, and act as if you didn't see them. It's the same in any communication when we choose to avoid, distract, or ignore what the other person is saying.

Instead of listening and talking about what the other person wants, we sidetrack and divert the topic. It's as though we dropped a detour right into the middle of the conversation. We do whatever we can to avoid the issue altogether, sending the message that we really aren't interested in talking about it at all. There are a number of ways we do this, but each has the same motive—changing the subject.

Whether you do it blatantly by a sudden head turn, subtly by reassuring the other person, or logically by proposing a solution to their problem, the person's feelings are ignored. They soon get the message not to share anything profound or significant with you as it will be pushed to the side. Kain Ramsay says, "It's impossible to achieve genuine connection when you engage in avoidant behavior" (2022).

Here are just a few statements used to divert conversations:

- "You'll be fine; it's not a big deal…"
- "Speaking of that, let me tell you about…"
- "You think that's bad; I was…"
- "I don't want to talk about that now…"
- "I'm sure it'll all work out…"

Bella was a star at doing this. She had a quick answer for every situation, all designed to switch the conversation back to what she was most comfortable talking about—herself. Instead of really listening to her friends, everyone else's issues were ignored or glossed over. As a result, they preferred sharing deep, personal things between themselves when Bella wasn't around.

The best way to learn not to use this tactic is to be present in the conversation and actively listen. Listen beyond what's being said. Don't make it about you. Bella had to work really hard at staying with the conversation, and she's improving all the time.

There can be many different ways these obstacles pop up, but they're like flashing neon signs on a detour in the road, saying to others in the conversation, "Watch out, they don't really care about you!"

Choosing the right words can be tricky. At times, we might be so distracted because we're focused so hard on saying the appropriate thing at the right moment we miss out on the entire conversation. Take your time; you don't become wise, knowing all the right things to say overnight. It takes constant practice.

Wise words satisfy like a good meal; the right words bring satisfaction.
—Proverbs 18:20 NLT

NON-VERBAL ROADBLOCKS

*Watch those around you, take notice of your own actions, and
make your life better by understanding others and yourself better.*
—Brian Scott

Taking a few tips from the FBI handbook on how to read people
can help when you're talking to others. Politicians, lawyers, and
business leaders around the world hire body language experts to
help them read others and communicate better without using words
(PsychCentral, 2021). It's essential to follow and understand to
interpret better what's being "spoken" between people.

Just as we saw how your body language can show you're actively
listening to another person, it can also reveal when you're not
interested or don't want to be part of a conversation. What you do
with your arms, legs, hands, eyes, and facial expressions sends loud
and clear messages about whether you're involved. It's good to be able
to read these signs in others, so you can pick up how they're really
feeling toward your discussion. However, it's also essential to become
aware of your own non-verbal body cues, such as how you sit, stand,
or act. Could you be ending conversations early just because you're
unaware of your own non-verbal cues?

By picking up on these cues, you can avoid uncomfortable
confrontations and even be able to turn bad discussions into good
ones. Let's look at some of the more common forms of closed body
language that can cause a conversation to go off the road.

- **Blading**

    If you're on the defense, closing off your body to an attack,
    then chances are you're blading. You can see this performed
    in the sport of fencing or boxing, where the opponent stands

in such a way to protect themselves but is still engaged, ready for action. By standing with one foot forward and the rest of the body slightly turned away, leaning on the dominant foot stepped backward, you present only one side of your body.

It exposes less of your body, keeping all your vital parts protected. It could mean the other person disagrees with you and is getting ready for a fight—maybe not a physical one, but they're still on defense. This noticeable shift in the way a person is standing can put a stop to a friendly conversation, turning it into an argument.

- **Crossed Ankles**

   Just like a gate, you're being closed off by the other person when this happens. Whether they're sitting or standing, if one foot goes over the ankle lying on top of the other, then the conversation has hit a roadblock.

   This posture signals they're anxious or defensive. In an experiment at a dentist's office, 89% of the patients locked their ankles when they sat to get their teeth done, and 98% did this just before an injection (Van Edwards, 2021). The tighter the ankles are together, the stronger the stress signal indicating they're closed off from the conversation.

   There are a few exceptions, like when girls might cross their ankles while wearing a dress, but they don't usually keep that posture throughout. Also, if someone's sitting with their legs stretched out, and one foot is over the other, it's most likely they're very comfortable and not stressed.

- **Crossed Arms**

How often have you done this when your parents are about to lecture you about what you should or shouldn't have done in a particular situation? It's a natural way of blocking ourselves from what's being said. We fold our arms like a gate, like a roadblock.

In an experiment, half a group was told to sit with arms and legs unfolded during a series of presentations, while the other half had to sit with arms crossed. Those who folded their arms remembered 38% less of what was said during the lectures (Van Edwards, 2021).

Known as the "self-hug," it's a way of showing anger, stress, or anxiety. It's not a helpful way to conduct a conversation, especially a casual one, as it may send the wrong message.

- **See No Evil, Hear No Evil, Speak No Evil**

In the same manner, the three monkeys sit, one covering their eyes, one covering their ears, and one covering their mouth; these are clues we've closed down the conversation. Naturally, we don't sit with our hands over our eyes, ears, and mouth, but we fidget, rub, scratch, yawn, and place our hands on our faces.

Unless you have allergies, these continual, slight hand movements to the eyes, ears, and mouth signal you're anxious. Rubbing your eyes acts as both a way to calm down when something isn't going well or an attempt to cut off eye contact to avoid stress or difficult topics. Touching your ears, according to Biologist Nikolaas Tinbergen, is a method of easing the tension, especially when you've been publicly embarrassed (Van Edwards, 2021). Continually rubbing the mouth sends similar messages of unease.

In an interrogation, any of these movements are significant cues that the person being questioned is under stress, anxious, and potentially even lying.

- **Excessive Nodding**

Nodding the head too often isn't normal. That individual isn't necessarily agreeing with the fantastic things you're saying. They may be overly nervous or just want to have a chance to speak! They may be lost in the conversation and just want you to stop talking so they can catch up in their mind. They may lack the confidence to say stop out loud. So by shaking their head a lot, they're trying to win your favor by agreeing with everything you're saying in the hope you'll stop talking.

In a normal, casual conversation between friends, there should never be an overdose of nodding; otherwise, something's wrong.

- **Furrowed Eyebrows**

Micro-expressions are important when reading what the other person is really saying. These can be easy to miss because they're not as obvious as crossed legs or arms, but they're just as important. One example is when the forehead wrinkles, pushing the eyebrows together. It's a sign your listener is confused or uneasy about something.

When you notice this, it indicates the person listening is stuck thinking about something, and the conversation cannot continue freely. Furrowed eyebrows are a negative sign, warning you something is wrong.

- **Fidgeting**

  Nervous? Watch your hands and how the fingers start moving, grabbing each other, fiddling with the chair, the clothes, the phone, anything. It's a subliminal action of searching for something more stimulating and exciting. Fidgeting shows boredom, and if that's what you're seeing in the other person as you're speaking, it's not good. They're bored with the conversation and probably with you as well.

  It can also mean the person is uneasy, as research on people about to board a flight across the Atlantic showed 80% of the passengers fiddled with wallets, tickets, and baggage (Van Edwards, 2021). If you want a clear, open conversation, be sure to keep your hands from fidgeting.

- **Too Much or Too Little Eye Contact**

  We all need to show eye contact, especially when we're engaged in a conversation. This means looking at the other person's eyes for short periods and then looking away. Timing is critical as too long can indicate one thing, while too short can mean something entirely different.

  Try staring at someone without warning. Watch what they do. They will get uncomfortable or may even get irritated. They may sense you as a threat or a stalker. Staring is not normal behavior. It can be perceived as you trying to dominate them. Even if you don't glare at the person, just looking at them too long could be read as you're interested in them in a flirty way.

The opposite is also true, as too little eye contact can be read as suspicious. It could indicate the person is shy, submissive, or even lying. You would need to know them a little bit before casting a judgment, especially about lying. Also, you must recognize and understand the meaning of eye contact differs significantly between cultures. Regardless, little or no eye contact with the speaker can quickly stall a conversation, just like coming to a red traffic light.

The eye is the lamp of the body. —Matthew 6:22 ESV

Alex's body language was all wrong in conversations. He would cross his arms and legs as well as avoid anyone's gaze from behind his curtain of hair. No wonder people didn't or couldn't have any meaningful discussions with him. He made it almost impossible right from the start.

It was not easy for him to wrench his feet apart, lift his head, and look another person in the face. He had to practice and even went so far as to ask a close friend to record him while they were in a conversation. Blake Eastman suggests this as an excellent way to see you for who you are while talking to others and says that "Raw behavioral data—displayed via video—is the reality of what's happening" (2021).

Alex's transformation created by just a few simple body language changes was astounding. Instead of a barrier of roadblocks, the road was open, allowing conversations to happen.

Ethan is not shy like Alex. He's not afraid to say what he thinks, sometimes too much! He had to learn not to glare at others. Softening his stare, looking away a few times without becoming shifty, actually made him more charming. Girls began to notice the color in his eyes, not his intense gaze.

Once again, it takes some practice, but little by little, habit by habit, each one of us can learn how to improve and remove these obstacles from our conversations.

HELPING SOMEONE ELSE

"Kindness and helping others will return to you when
you least expect it, and maybe when you need it."
—*Catherine Pulsifer*

Remember Alex, the boy I told you about in the introduction? He was riddled with anxiety, insecurity, and self-doubt… Perhaps much like you were when you picked up this book. But what he had in his favor was that he was able to reach out and ask for help.

That was a difficult thing for him to do, but he was able to… and not everyone is. I know I wasn't when I was his age.

As I worked with Alex, he began to realize that he wasn't alone and that there were people in his life who wanted to help him. Through the skills and techniques I taught him—the very ones you're picking up as you work your way through this book—he gradually became a happier and more confident version of himself… and it is my hope that the same thing will happen to you.

But what about those people who don't have the confidence to reach out and ask for help, those who feel like they're the only one going through this and that they have to hide it?

Well, this is your opportunity to help them.

By leaving a review of this book on Amazon, you'll show other young people that they're not alone and that there's a way for them to grow their confidence and find their place in the world.

Simply by letting other readers know how this book has helped you and what they'll find inside, you'll show them where they can find the guidance they need—and you'll demonstrate that they're not the only person who feels this way.

Thank you for your help. When you're struggling with your self-confidence, asking for help can be extremely difficult... With your support, I can help even those who aren't able to ask for it.

SIX
Engaging in Casual Conversation

The great thing is to know when to speak and when to keep quiet.
—Seneca the Younger

Jamal loves his phone! It's not just a great distraction from the pressures of school and life, but it's an easy way to communicate with anyone and everyone. And the best part is he doesn't have to worry about awkward pauses, the tone of his voice, or sending the wrong body language messages. Jamal can control every single word.

It sounds almost perfect, especially when spontaneous, spur-of-the-moment communication can be so overwhelming. When we're not so sure of ourselves or our conversational skills, then stepping out might seem like a scary choice. But true friendships aren't built on GIFs, memes, or emojis. They start with casual conversations—chatting about everything and nothing.

Jamal had to learn there were things that he couldn't say, couldn't see, couldn't be part of from behind a screen. By learning the skills and techniques we've looked at so far in this book, he has been able to put his phone on silent, stick it in his pocket, and have face-to-face conversations. Jamal still loves his phone, but he has found genuine laughter shared with others goes much deeper and is far more satisfying than a clever emoji!

CASUAL CONVERSATIONS

It's not the rehearsed speech in a class presentation or the carefully crafted words we use when we meet *that* boy or girl for the first time. Casual means it's light, fun, and can flow from topic to topic. Nobody really knows what to say next. That's what makes it interesting—and sometimes scary!

Sharing stories and jokes, these chats are often filled with slang and words an adult might not understand. It's relaxed and informal. Instead of staring at each other in silence, casual conversations can fill the gap. It's the easiest and best way to build relationships with people.

But what happens when you're stuck with someone you don't know that well? What do you talk about? Are there any ways to navigate the awkward silences that pop up in these moments? How do you start and not fall on your face? What do you say to keep the train from derailing? Is there a way to finish without running away as if you've just witnessed a murder? Let's look at some tips and tricks.

Starting

Opening a casual conversation can sometimes be the most challenging part, especially when it's with people you hardly know or don't know at all. The last thing you want is to make a fool of yourself. With a few handy conversation starters up your sleeves, you can step up and make contact!

- **Awkward Reveal**

  Starting is always the hardest—how to begin the conversation? Instead of hiding behind feeling awkward, you can break the ice by admitting it. Shari Leid, the author of *The 50/50 Friendship Flow*, says, "When we focus on not being awkward, we become more awkward" (Brabham, 2022). By being honest, it opens the door for the other person to walk into the conversation. They're probably feeling exactly the same way you are.

- **Complimentary Starter**

  Everyone loves a compliment, so what better way to start than by acknowledging the other person's clothes, hair, or phone? Leid says, "It can help get you out of your head. It shows the person you see them, you notice them" (Brabham, 2022). Start with something like, "I really like your shirt; where did you get it?" "Your hair looks great; who did it for you?" or "That's a cool phone cover; when did you get it?"

  Notice the unique complement starter structure; a question always follows the compliment, allowing the chat to begin.

- **Pop Quiz**

  People like to talk about themselves. Give the other person a chance to tell you something personal by asking questions like "Who's your favorite YouTuber or TikToc at the moment?" "What are you doing this weekend?" "What's your favorite sport?" "What's your favorite Netflix series?" "Do you enjoy this weather?" "Who's your favorite superhero?" The list is endless of what you could ask.

It's important not to judge them on their answer, even if you don't agree or don't like their choice of YouTuber, TicToc, sport, or superhero. That will shut down a conversation before it begins. Let them have their opinion, and feel free to respond with your favorite YouTuber, TicToc, sport, or superhero. You might not agree, but it will create an opportunity to discuss the topic further.

- **Clever Launch**

  Rather than sticking to the usual "How are you?" question, you could try a more expansive approach by asking, "What's on your mind?" "What emoji do you feel like right now?" or "What three words describe your day so far?"

  Most people just answer "fine" when asked how they are, even if they're not. You might spark a more honest answer by asking different questions like these, setting off a very different conversation.

Continuing

Now that you've got your chat started, how do you ensure it keeps going? There are many ways to make sure your talk doesn't run out of steam. Here are some handy tips to recharge a dying conversation.

- **Common Ground**

  Finding something that fascinates both of you is the best way to keep a conversation from running out of gas. Whether it's movies, fashion, or sports, a common interest will be a great connection and give you lots to talk about. Ask a few questions to see what the other person enjoys, and then go from there.

- **Small Talk**

Only talking about what's one thing, like the weather or a YouTuber, can be a bit awkward, but don't be too quick to try and steer the conversation into something deeper. Small talk can be very useful to continue the chat until you discover some common interests.

Christopher Gottschalk writes in his book, *How to Start and Make a Conversation,* jumping too quickly from small talk to a deep conversation "results in you getting too personal before the other person is comfortable with you" (The Cut, 2020). S0, don't stress. Take your time and let the conversation find its way to the next topic without forcing it.

- **Repeat and Absorb**

This is a clever little trick to show you're listening, and it can set you up to ask another question or for the other person to respond. By repeating their answer in your own words and thinking aloud about it, you show you're genuinely interested. It makes the other person's answer the main topic and also allows them to feel very important.

Here's an example of how not to do this. Notice how the speaker only replies with their own view rather than understanding the other person's opinion out loud.

OTHER: "I loved living in California. It's so warm."

SPEAKER: "You lived in California? I was not fond of the weather there. It was too hot and sticky."

Now, let's see how the speaker could have used this information to repeat it back in an open, friendly way.

OTHER: "I loved living in California. It was always so warm."

SPEAKER: "You lived in California? It must have been great growing up in such a climate..."

It's all about acknowledging the other person and allowing them the opportunity to share *before* giving your opinions.

- **Driving FORD**

This is another clever way to remember safe small-talk topics for causal conversations. Family, Occupation, Recreation, and Dreams are easy and familiar to everyone. Family, Occupation (or school), and Recreation are quick, easy, and reliable topics that can jumpstart any conversation. Dreams, passions, and interests can bridge a chat toward a more profound, intimate, and revealing exchange.

- **Open-Ended Questions**

A good open-ended question creates more conversation and can keep it going for a long time. Gottschalk calls this the "ripple theory of conversation" because it's like dropping a pebble into water, creating ripples of more things to talk about (The Cut, 2020).

Instead of closed questions like, "Do you like football?" that only has a yes or no answer, you can ask, "How do you feel about playing or watching football?" The difference in your wording allows the other person to take the lead, decide what they want to share, and go from there. Other good open-ended questions include:

"How was your day?"

"How do you feel about that?"

"What are you going to do now?"

"Tell me about you."

- **Dig Deeper**

There will be moments when you can ditch the small talk and ask more personal questions. Listen carefully for these times using your best active listening techniques and observing their body language to determine if they're ready to go to the next level. Good questions to ask to get the ball rolling toward a more profound conversation include:

"Who's your hero/role model?"

"What do you worry about the most?" or

"What did you always want to be?"

Try the **IFR** method to ensure you don't turn your chat into a police interrogation!

Inquire—ask a question.

Follow-up—find out a bit more about their answer.

Relate—share something to keep the conversation balanced.

- **Keep It Going**

Here are a few questions that can really get a conversation going. They'll make you think, reveal something about yourself and the person you're chatting with, and even bring some laughter to your discussion.

1. How long would you last in a zombie apocalypse?
2. If you had an intro song that played every time you walked into a room, what would it be?
3. If you had to change your name, what would your new name be?
4. If you got three wishes from a genie, what would they be?
5. What superpower do you wish you always had?
6. If you could travel anywhere in the world, where would you go?
7. What food represents you the most?
8. How do you feel about pineapple on pizza?
9. If you were immortal for a day, what would you do?
10. What food do you avoid at all costs?

(Ives, 2022)

- **Enjoying the Crickets**

For some reason, we're all afraid of silence—hearing nothing but crickets chirping in the night! Remember, casual conversations aren't meant to be structured or linear, moving from point A to point B. They should have a life of their own, finding their own route depending on who's involved.

Part of normal conversations is silence, moments when there's nothing more to say on the topic. Remember, you're not the only one in the conversation. Each person involved has the same amount of responsibility to keep a conversation going. So, give it some time before you try to force everyone to carry on talking.

Ending

You stepped out, made contact, and somehow kept it going, but how do you stop it before it drives over a cliff, pulling everyone down with it? These are a few tried-and-tested maneuvers you can sneak into the conversation to get you out.

- **Thanks**

  If you've had enough and you need to leave, sometimes the best way to cut a conversation is simply to be direct. "It was great chatting with you, but I need to get going" is a decent line to use. You compliment the other person, leaving them feeling good about themselves, and even seal the chat with a handshake, fist bump, or hug to say goodbye.

- **Excuse**

  We all have to end conversations at some point, so don't feel bad. You're not the only one. Dr. Westbrook, a psychiatrist, says, "Being comfortable with ending conversations can help maintain rapport in a relationship." (Miller, 2021). Getting frustrated with other people because we don't know how to finish a chat can put them off.

  One way to get out of a conversation is to excuse yourself. It can be a legitimate one or a made-up one. "Can you excuse me? I need to go to the bathroom," "Excuse me, but I did want to go and meet so-and-so," or "I'm sorry, I really have to get going. I promised so-and-so I would be there." You can say you need to call someone or say you're going to grab something to eat or drink, and you'll see them later.

- **Ask**

  Put the responsibility on the other person by asking them to recommend where you should go or who you should see next. If you're at a party, ask them who else they think you should go and meet. You could ask them to recommend the best place for you to get something to eat or drink nearby. Any question where it tells them you're about to move on at their suggestion will work.

There's no formula that works every time. Each conversation is unique. The people are different, the circumstances change, how you're feeling isn't the same every time, and what you talk about will vary. It's not about getting it right 100% of the time. It's about getting better, feeling more confident, and building relationships. That means there'll be moments where it might fall flat, no matter what techniques you try.

Jamal made a number of mistakes when he first tried to have casual conversations. He pushed too hard, trying to create conversations out of thin air. He asked too many questions when he was worried the conversation was dying. He played with his phone without knowing, putting the other person off. He wanted to give up.

But the great thing about Jamal is he didn't give up. He tried again and again, finding that with each new experience, he became more comfortable steering and helping the conversation move along through each new chat. There are still times he prefers putting his thoughts and feelings into a neat, clever text, but now he looks forward to conversations where it's all about the journey, not knowing where it might lead.

EXERCISE

Rate yourself against these statements as honestly as possible to see how good you are at casual conversations. Remember being overconfident and not confident in these moments can be issues you need to learn to overcome.

Score yourself for each statement with the following answers:

0—Rarely or never

1—Occasionally

2—Often

3—I'm excellent at this, doing it consistently.

_____ 1. I often ask open-ended questions like *"How"* and *"What"* to discover more about the other person.

_____ 2. I show I'm listening by repeating and building on what the other person said.

_____ 3. I try not to use the word *"but"* when answering and rather use the word *"and"* in my sentences.

_____ 4. I avoid saying negative comments like *"I don't like..."* or *"That isn't..."*

_____ 5. I make sure everyone gets a chance to speak in a conversation, not just me.

_____ 6. I like to ask questions about the other person's life, viewpoints, and interests.

_____ 7. I can give information and ask questions.

_____ 8. I casually jump into conversations to add energy to them when it looks like they're dying out.

     9.   I sit up or stand tall and connect with my eyes, ears, and brain, as well as with words.

    10. I'm interested in others and in the world around me.
(Heltler, 2015)

How did you do in this assessment of your friendly chatting skills? If your overall score was 20 or above, you're probably in good shape. If it's below 20, the techniques you've read about and learned to practice will improve your skills. The closer you are to 30, the better you are as a conversationalist.

Being good at conversations doesn't just happen. There's no genie that will make you an overnight chat star. Even if you're good at talking and have no problem with words, it doesn't make you a great conversationalist. There are techniques you can learn to open the discussion, make others feel included, and keep the dialogue going. Whether you're happy to jump in and have your say, or you're afraid of making that first move, these tips and tricks can help you to form an excellent base to build your casual conversation skills.

You can always practice with a friend in your room, or maybe with one of your parents. It might seem a bit odd to role-play a conversation, but if you want to get better, then acting it out and trying a few of the techniques from this chapter is the best way to learn.

Words from the mouth of the wise are gracious,
but fools are consumed by their own lips.
—Ecclesiastes 10:12 NIV

SEVEN
The Brain and Hormones

Students get diplomas when they graduate from high school, but I think they should also get diplomas for simply surviving the teen years.
—Melanie Willard

Alex had another reason for growing the flop of hair that covered most of his face—acne. Through his years in junior high, he was generally happy, even though he didn't look for conversations or engage in every sport available. He had always been slightly reserved right from being a toddler. But the changes in his body pushed him even further into the shadows.

He washed his face every day as his mom instructed, and he tried to stay away from greasy foods, but the minefield of craters and volcanoes was hard to contain. It wasn't just his complexion. Every time he spoke, his voice dropped a few octaves mid-sentence like a weird musical experiment.

And then there were all these emotions—anger, loneliness, insecurity, and so many more all at once or out of the blue.

No wonder he snapped at his mom when she innocently asked if he had had a good day at school. He didn't mean to; it just happened. And it was happening more regularly.

The changes a teenage body goes through are no small event—they're massive, setting you up to be an adult. Everything changes—your body is a house going through a major renovation that lasts a few years! Understanding some of these alterations can help you navigate your way through them, not fight them or let them get the better of you. You don't have to wait until the remodeling is over. You can have a say in it now!

THE BRAIN

The teenage years from about 12 to 20, are when the brain undergoes natural surgery. Significant changes are happening. New neural connections are growing while others no longer used are cut back. It's the way the brain is being formed to become a more efficient "adult mental machine" (Davis, 2015). Like a tree is pruned in certain sections and allowed to sprout in others, so the brain is cultivated and grown. But it's not a smooth process. There are significant adjustments to be made. A lot of this is linked to hormonal changes, but we'll look at that later.

- **Amygdala**

    The brain is complex, but it can be divided into large pieces like a 3D puzzle. The prefrontal cortex is where all the planning takes place, sorting through information from other parts of the brain. Then there's the hippocampus, where memory happens, and finally, the amygdala—the area involved with emotions.

You guessed it, one of the main areas in the brain where all this intense remodeling is taking place is called the amygdala. White matter is growing in this section, and axons (neural transmitters) are stretching out to form new connections (Davis, 2015). While the other parts of the brain are transforming, the amygdala is in charge, and it doesn't always get it right.

Apart from being the place dealing with emotions, it's also responsible for sending out warnings. And just like a newly installed fire alarm, it sometimes malfunctions, sending out false alerts. That's why everything during the teenage years feels like a crisis! The amygdala triggers the fight-or-flight response, a lightning-quick decision on whether to withdraw or to stand up for yourself (Alton, 2019).

Because the amygdala is also going through a restructure, it can misfire, resulting in Alex suddenly snapping at his mom and then, without warning, retreating behind his hair. It's also why Ethan is so argumentative, as his amygdala is on red alert the whole time.

• **Hippocampus**

The one upside to an overactive amygdala is its impact on the hippocampus, located right next door, which becomes overstimulated by its neighbor's overactivity. This is good because the hippocampus deals with memory. More stimulation, more memory! So, as a teenager, you're able to learn fast and retain information more quickly.

The parts in control of speech are also affected. They're developing but have not yet reached their optimum level, only having about 75% of the adult words they need (Home-Start, 2020). Teenagers can understand the meanings behind sarcasm, idioms, euphemisms, and other ways of saying something with a double connotation, but they're still growing in the area of small talk. Even though Alex just grunts a one-syllable answer, and we think he may not be developing past the Stone Age, his brain is rapidly increasing in vocabulary.

It doesn't mean they have all the words. The connections being created in the brain are still new, so often, while the words to respond exist, they don't always find their way to the mouth. The result is a standard three-word answer to almost any question. When asked, "How was your day?" many connections need to be fired instantaneously, but instead of a decent response, it rolls out as "I don't know." What you really mean is, "I can't find, access, and deliver the words required to express my true answer."

Take heart; this will rapidly change with time, and the words will overflow in endless bounty. Trying to express yourself can be painful because not all the things you want to say are there yet. Your words and mental connections are getting there, and with time you will reach a comfortable place where you can express exactly what's on your mind with the right words quickly.

- **Prefrontal Cortex**

As if all these aren't enough, there's another area also going through changes. The prefrontal cortex, the central processing unit, is being rewired to be able to handle more complex issues as well as deal with hormones. It's also the part dealing with impulses and consequences.

The prefrontal cortex is the last area of the brain to develop. This remodeling starts from the back and works toward the front, where the prefrontal cortex is situated. This is why teens are often quite reckless, not worried about what'll happen next. It's why they can be suddenly aggressive, switching behavior without a moment's notice.

THE HORMONES

Tiana feels out of her depth. Every day is like drifting into outer space, not knowing if she'll find a hospitable and kind planet or a hostile one filled with molten lava. One moment, she feels like her feet are firmly on the ground, and she can do this. The next moment, she's floating out of control with no assurance she'll make it back to earth. And to make matters worse, she likes a dreamy boy in class, and she's not sure what to do about it or if it's true love!

As a teen, you will go through something similar. Your hormones are constantly changing, sending weird messages sometimes of intense emotion, then suddenly dropping off entirely, and you suddenly don't care about anything. It's an unending roller coaster!

The main hormones are estrogen and testosterone. These don't just affect emotions but cause changes in the body as well. A sudden growth spurt and facial hair in boys while girls experience menstruation. These are just some of the reactions within your body caused by the hormonal shift. These hormones are known as "sex steroids" because they are produced in the genital region, and they dramatically increase during puberty (Davis, 2015).

- **Self-Esteem**

Just like Alex and his acne dilemma, Tiana suddenly became obsessed with the way she looked when she was in a crowd and even on her own. She wanted to be herself but not stand out too much. She worried about her hair, her weight, her shoes… everything! This self-consciousness is a normal effect of hormonal changes and is greatly amplified by social media.

Becoming aware of who you are and your identity is a critical element in becoming a healthy, well-grounded teenager. It's not just your personality but the music you listen to, the clothes you wear, the social media you follow, and even the friends you hang out with; they all play a part in defining who you are as a person. There's so much pressure to fit in, and often, it can feel like you're losing some of who you are just to follow the latest social trend.

Not only is it a necessary time to figure out who you are and where your place in society is, but it's also a critical time to learn how to speak to friends and family in conversations without being childish.

When I was a child, I spoke and thought and reasoned as a child. But when I grew up, I put away childish things.
—1 Corinthians 13:11 NLT

- **Taking Risks**

New experiences rank high on your list of priorities. Often these are linked with taking bigger risks for more incredible thrills, trying to fill the increased need for dopamine (Home-Start, 2020). With the prefrontal cortex still developing, its capacity to understand consequences is muffled so that often things are done without thinking. There's a tendency to create a "bulletproof" mentality as though nothing can hurt you, and you will live forever (Tozer, 2016). The decision-making apparatus is not fully functioning, sometimes leading to poor choices.

All these result in more risks being taken to enjoy life no matter what the consequences! While stepping out and trying new things can be healthy, learning where your limits are can be a harsh life lesson.

- **More Responsibility**

Becoming an adult means standing up for yourself. There are areas at home and school where you want to step out on your own and take charge of your decisions. This may involve greater responsibility at home or school as you struggle to forge your own choices and deal with both the joys and consequences of those decisions.

It's an essential step to becoming an individual and a grown-up. Having some measure of authority in a group project or a team means a lot at this age.

- **Sexual Identity**

With all the hormones raging around the body, it's no surprise romantic relationships become a massive part of most teens' lives at this point. This is not necessarily sexual contact or intimate connections but a definite shift toward "more than friends!"

With pressure and misinformation from social media, the internet, and peers, it can be challenging to form a healthy sexual identity. The increase in estrogen in girls or testosterone in boys complicates the brain's ability to stay calm and focused, especially when you're face to face with someone you "really like."

- **Understanding Right From Wrong**

  While the prefrontal cortex is still under construction, your conscience formed by the examples around you helps balance your understanding of what is right or wrong. You rely on your brain to process information, even with raging hormones tempting you to lean into your feelings rather than stepping back to allow your conscience to guide your decisions. Social media triggers your hormones creating conflict to influence your choices. It's important to understand that none of your favorite Social Influencers ever has to answer for even a single choice they cause you to make.

  Allowing your emotions to sway your judgments makes these choices very confusing. In conversations, remember to use the "I feel" statements to avoid getting caught off guard when someone challenges your feelings rather than stating what they think. Figuring out the line between your emotions and your choices can be very tricky.

- **Importance of Friends**

  As a teenager, there's a subtle but distinct shift in your social world. Your peers, social media, and the internet become more critical influencers in your life. You begin to branch out from your parents and family. You're on a mission to discover who you are. Friends, social media, and other significant adults begin to affect how you see yourself and the world around you as you grow into a more independent person. You're forming your own views, developing your own relationships, and making your own decisions. All of these play a critical role in your independent growth process.

The need for growth can lead to friction with parents as you strive to break free from your family structure to spend more time with friends. Developing new friendships can also be challenging as you try to form bonds with others who might not always think or act as you do. Dealing with these social changes can seem tricky, but there are things you can do to ensure you communicate your desires in a healthy manner. We have discussed many options around this subject in the previous chapters.

As you better understand the changes brewing inside you and test techniques to help you navigate your developing hormonal and body changes, the journey ahead becomes easier to navigate. It can become a rewarding experience that allows you to strive to become more confident in yourself, your friendships, and your relationships.

EXERCISE

Let's take a moment and review your understanding of your brain, hormones, and the challenges you face. See if you can answer these true or false questions. Remember, even a wrong answer is an opportunity to learn!

Questions

1. Teens are "young adults" because their brain development gives them adult skills, although they lack the experience of older adults. **T F**

2. The teenage brain has less matter in the areas that control planning and problem-solving. That's why teens make bad choices. **T F**

3. Teenagers stay up late because they require less sleep than adults. **T F**

4. Teens seem emotionally sensitive because they respond to subtle cues that adults miss. **T F**

5. Teenagers should not blame their bad behavior on "raging hormones." **T F**

6. The teenage brain develops in such a way promoting impulsive and risk-taking activities. **T F**

7. Parents don't have much influence on teens because their brain development makes them more sensitive to social cues from their peers. **T F**

8. You have the brain you are born with, and there's not much you can do about it. **T F**

Answers

1. False. In brain development, a complete "young adult" brain is reached at the age of 25. The brain is still developing from the teenage years to the early 20s. Some areas are growing more complex, while others are cutting back, removing unused connections, and strengthening links between several regions. While many cognitive functions are similar in adolescents and adults, they do not function in the same manner.

2. False. The last process for the adolescent brain to mature involves the "pruning" of nerve cell material, not adding more. New connections are being made, but unused circuits are also being cut out. As adolescents grow, the active connections are coated with myelin, helping information flow more quickly and efficiently. It's like a computer doing massive parallel processing functions rather than one using a single processing function.

3. False. Adolescents require more sleep than adults—about nine hours—and they tend to go to sleep at later hours and wake up later. Research shows this to be accurate, but the biological mechanisms for these differences are still not understood.

4. False. Teens have less capacity to recognize anger in facial images than adults. It means brain areas necessary for processing subtle changes in facial expressions are still developing in adolescents. Teens might be more emotional because the parts of their brains that control social interactions develop earlier than the areas that deal with overreactions.

5. True. Puberty often begins before the teenage years, with hormonal changes peaking at ages 12 to 15. Hormones then balance out, reaching adult levels by the age of 18. Blaming your behavior on hormones or your still-developing brain

not yet capable of adequately regulating behavior does not stop you from facing the consequences of your actions. In the end, you are still responsible for your actions, no matter how you felt at the time!

6. True. The human brain circuits anticipating good things develop before the circuits that anticipate all the consequences of those actions. Remember, you will still face the consequences of your actions regardless of what your brain tells you.

7. False. Studies in biotechnology show teens take greater risks when they are with their peers than when they are alone (Chein et al., 2011). However, research also shows that parents can significantly influence teens' attitudes and behaviors.

8. False. Studies reveal the structure of the brain changes with experience. The ability to use parts of your brain changes over time. People who learn to play a musical instrument, dance, sing, master video games, study science, engineering, and architecture, read books, participate in plays, master communication skills, and develop social connections all form different brain connections. And as you improve any skill, your brain grows and becomes more efficient at the task.

(USNews, 2008)

Adolescence is an enormous shift from being a child to becoming an adult. There's so much going on in the brain, the body, the hormones, and all around you at the same time. It can be daunting to face daily, especially when you're unsure of your emotions. We are all human so no one will be on top of things 100% of the time. An argument or even the slightest eye roll can quickly topple an otherwise great day. One single nasty word can destroy your upbeat, happy mood. Friends can become enemies instantly over mixed feelings.

Your teen years may be filled with fear, worry, and anger. Still, they are the beginning of an incredible journey toward joyful friends, amazing adventures, beautiful moments, and lasting relationships. Learning to properly communicate and listen to those around you can spare you from any curveballs your hormones may throw. Understanding how your brain and body develop is helpful as you implement the previous chapters' communication techniques to navigate any twists and turns. Finally, knowing there are people to walk alongside you in times of need can help you steer your ship in any stormy water!

EIGHTH
It Starts at Home

Home is where one starts from.
—T. S. Eliot

Ethan was arguing again! His mom and dad were trying to organize the weekend and plan something special for the family. They had their ideas, and Ethan had his. A stalemate happened as both Ethan and his parents dug their heels in and stopped listening to each other. Ethan wasn't even sure what he wanted! Instead of talking about what they could do together, they ended up yelling about everything they never got to do. They covered every past weekend's failed plans. Ethan's dad lost his cool, so a simple discussion blew up into a full-blown heated battle before they knew it.

Ethan has a good family. His dad works hard, doing his best to set aside time for his son, practicing sports or engaging in games. His mom makes sure Ethan has what he needs for food, clothing, school, and after-school activities, all while playing taxi to every one of Ethan's events. She even slips a note of encouragement and treats into his lunch every so often. Ethan really loves his parents. He sees how much they sacrifice for him. But arguments and misunderstandings have become common over the past year. Since Ethan stepped into his teenage sneakers, it seems like the three of them can't agree on anything. The peace and happiness that once filled their home has been replaced by silence, scowls, frowns, and constant storms.

Fortunately, this is not a doom and gloom situation. It's not as though there's no way back for Ethan's family. Arguments in any household are normal, with or without teenagers! Not everyone shares your way of thinking or sees things the way you do, so there will always be disagreements. In fact, only 5–15% of teens display extreme rebellion, go through major earthquake-shifting conflicts with their parents, or suffer off-the-charts emotional turmoil (Tozer, 2016). Most of you are not in the 15%, so what we experience is normal.

Most conflicts can be resolved by stepping back and using a few simple techniques.

Ethan learned to take a breath when the heat rushed up his neck. Before he launched into an attack, he counted to himself and tried looking at things from his parent's perspective. His mom and dad weren't always right about the way they spoke, so they also focused on improving their communication methods. Instead of pointing out what each one did or didn't do, they all tried to stick to talking about their requirements, needs, and wants. Instead of feelings of frustration, betrayal, and hate, they've been focusing on all the positive emotions they feel for each other.

Ethan's been playing his part. It doesn't always work. His dad's a bit of a hothead like him, and they have it out every so often. But they're quick to see where things are going, so they slow it down and use simple techniques to get the conversation back on track. The weather forecast now shows sunny patches, with no major storm fronts coming in the near future!

You might have a similar experience to Ethan. Or it might be like Tiana, who doesn't yell, but her muttering and angry eyes say just as much. Power struggles are a part of you becoming an adult, trying to find some space in a home where there's already an adult or two—trying to make your place as an individual. But it doesn't have to be a struggle; remember, you're not alone!

IT TAKES TWO

With any communication, it takes at least two to make it work! The skills in this book will help you understand yourself and grow as a healthy, confident teen. And the skills and techniques also work for those who are responsible for you at home. If your parents, guardians, or any adults read these chapters, they will also benefit. Not just by learning about what you're going through but also by adopting these same techniques to improve their communication style. Anyone can learn these techniques and improve their conversations, discussions, and social interactions.

We have added an appendix, especially for your parents or guardians, and nothing is stopping you from reading their section and them from reading yours. These sections are not exclusive and will help you see things from each other's perspectives. You could benefit from reading and discussing how you feel, what you learned, what you are willing to try, and your combined expectations from your experiments.

EXERCISE

First, let's see what life's like at your house. What happens during a conversation or an argument? Be honest. Don't hold back. It's good to see things the way they really are. Moms and dads take time to work through these as well. Healthy communication starts when you all take part in the process of acknowledging the way you act and react and then finding ways to improve.

Which of the following communication habits do you find yourself and your parents using with each other? There is no total score and no failure. The objective is honestly to recognize how you are in moments of communication. And if you can, without causing another argument, compare your answers with each other!

Indicate how often you use each one using a simple scale of
    1—little
    2—a lot

Questions

1. Use the words "always" and "never."   **1 2**
2. Yell, shout or raise your voice.   **1 2**
3. Tease or mock the other person.   **1 2**
4. Repeat your opinion constantly.   **1 2**
5. Threaten to do something if they don't listen.   **1 2**
6. Interrupt.   **1 2**
7. Give short, unhelpful responses: "Uh huh" or "I don't know."   **1 2**
8. Make suggestions.   **1 2**
9. Make demands.   **1 2**
10. Argue over minor points.   **1 2**

11. Talk very little, remain silent, or refuse to talk.   **1 2**

12. Talk a lot.   **1 2**

13. Joke.   **1 2**

14. Praise or compliment.   **1 2**

15. Ask what the other person would like.   **1 2**

16. Accuse or blame others.   **1 2**

17. Exaggerate how bad things are.   **1 2**

18. Talk in a sarcastic tone of voice.   **1 2**

19. Avoid using eye contact.   **1 2**

20. Dwell on the past, and tell stories of how it used   **1 2**
to be.

21. Call someone names or swear.   **1 2**

22. Use inappropriate hand gestures or make threats.   **1 2**

(UW, n.d.)

Remember, there are no right or wrong answers in this exercise. The objective is to reveal how you behave and speak to others in conversations or arguments. Just like standing in front of a mirror to see if your hair is out of place so you can put it right, adjust your clothes, or wipe the food from your mouth. The same clarity needs to happen for you to see your authentic self in a conversation. And instead of walking away from the mirror without doing anything, you can correct certain behaviors and improve.

Try this if you want to take a trip on the wild side. If you have a good relationship with your parents, guardians, or BFF, try repeating this exercise with one minor change. This time, fill out the answers based on how you hear the other person commonly respond in your joint discussions while they do the same for you. Now comes the moment of truth. Compare their responses to the questions to the answers you gave yourself. This kind of honesty can be genuinely revealing because these people are the actual mirrors of how you speak and act in conversations.

WHAT YOU CAN DO

If you want to change the world, go home, and love your family.
—Mother Teresa

You've seen a lot of different suggestions in this book about how you can improve various aspects of communication and the skills needed to become better communicators. They're all useless, though, until you actually try them out and start practicing. It's never too late to start, never too late to improve who you are. And the best place to start is right at home!

That's right. Try a few of these out on your parents, your siblings, or whoever else might be living there. It's as though your house has become your science lab, your family members, your test subjects, and you, the crazy professor! Let the experiments and research begin!

Experiment with everything you learned in the previous chapters. Here are some simple and practical suggestions to start with and introduce into your daily life and conversations. Don't try all of them at once. It will look staged, as though you're putting on a performance. Instead, take it one step at a time and make small changes daily or even weekly. After a while, you will begin to see small but significant improvements in your communication skills and in your overall confidence.

Think of this as an overall checklist of things to do in conversations.

- **Start Listening**

    No one understands you? Your parents just don't get you? You try your hardest to tell them how you feel, what you want, and who you are, but it's like talking to a wall. Nobody listens to you! When was the last time you stopped and took a moment to truly listen to *them*? You expect everyone to hear what you have to say, but it's not honest communication unless you also honor others by really listening to them. If you want to be heard, improve your active listening skills, and become a better listener.

Go back to Chapter 2 and see all the tips on how to listen actively. Start using them in your daily conversations, and you will begin to see positive changes. Whenever you're talking, if it's with your parents or friends, start listening to understand instead of just responding. If you're not sure about something, ask. Don't assume. Actively listening will help you avoid unnecessary misunderstandings and reduce conflicts. Even when you're just talking to someone over the phone, pay attention to the conversation instead of doing something else, like scrolling through your social media feeds.

- **Understand Your Audience**

The way you talk depends on who you're talking to. Your friends might understand the informal language you use or the inside jokes, but others may not. It would be best if you also thought about the age of those in your discussion. Using abbreviations like GTG or ICYMI will probably go straight over your parents' heads. Don't assume everyone knows and uses the same language, abbreviations, or slang you use. Adjust your words and reduce your slang to engage everyone you're talking to in the conversation.

- **Watch Body Language**

Remember that 90% of what is said isn't in the spoken words, so you have to be alert to all the non-verbal communication cues as well. Not just in others but from yourself too. If your verbal and non-verbal communication doesn't match, it can cause major confusion and lead to unnecessary conflicts and misunderstandings. This can be easily avoided by watching your body language.

While you're worrying about getting the words right, you also have to watch others' non-verbal signals. That's why learning to observe others' body language takes time and practice.

If you roll your eyes when your parents say something, it can trigger an argument. So, try and keep it from happening. Or if your mom corrects you on it, don't take it personally; she's actually helping out! If your parents seem upset and their body language shows you they are stressed, it might not be the right time to ask them about going to a concert. You will become a better communicator when you learn to properly interpret and use body language.

- **Check Everything**

  Communication isn't just spoken but written as well. If you're the queen or king of texting, and your thumbs are a blur as you type—be careful! Check what you've written *before* hitting send. It doesn't have to match your grammar teacher's standards, but it has to be clear and make sense to the person receiving it. This improves your communication skills and ensures what you've written is the intended message. If you're in the middle of an emotional exchange, it's better not to type out a long message opening up too many areas for miscommunication. Keep it short, to the point, and sensible.

  You can still be the king or queen of texting, just way better!

- **Just Call**

On the subject of texting, if there's a lot to be said, then don't type it! Make a phone or FaceTime call instead of sending long, elaborate text messages filled with words, emojis, and gifs. Texts might feel more manageable because you're in control of your conversation, but using your voice to convey your thoughts and feelings leaves less room for miscommunications. Direct messages on social media might seem like a good option at the time, but texting or chatting online doesn't compare to the genuine reality of a voice or FaceTime call. Pick up the phone and engage in a conversation. Directly talking to someone is also a great way to improve your verbal communication skills.

If it's something with mom, dad, or a friend, the relationship will be built faster and deeper through your spoken words than through any text!

- **Make a Note**

Notes are one of the easiest ways to improve your communication skills. Write down the different things you want to talk about. Start practicing this tip, whether it's a note on your phone or something written in a notebook. Too often, you think you can remember something, but by the time you get to it, you've forgotten what the thing was. By writing or making notes, your brain stores them for later use.

Having it in your memory makes it easier to bring up all the points or topics you want without missing anything important. This little habit also improves your ability to stay organized. So, when you're feeling overwhelmed by emotions, instead of talking, take a moment to make a note of what you're thinking and feeling. You might even find that what you felt was so important a few hours ago is suddenly not as crucial to bring up in your conversation any longer.

- **Stop and Think**

  Before you speak:

  1. Pause and think if you really need to say what you're about to say.
  2. Respect the other person regardless of who they are.
  3. If it takes a moment longer, you can even tell the other person to give you a minute to think about it. This will give you time to form the words in your mind and pay attention to what and how you say them. Reflecting on responses before talking, lets you decide whether it's best to say them or keep quiet.

This helps you regulate emotions and gather your thoughts.

It needs a bit of practice, especially if you're like Ethan and Bella, who speak before they think!

- **Stay Positive**

  By showing some confidence in the way you stand, sit, and speak, it doesn't just improve your communication skills; it makes it easier to stay positive, not letting your emotions take control. It would be best if you smiled as much as possible and made it genuine. Practicing in front of a mirror helps make this easier. When you smile, it puts others at ease and is contagious.

Would you rather go up to someone who's smiling or someone who's frowning? Don't you always check to see if your parents are in a good mood before asking for something? Stay positive and project positive emotions while talking, and your communication will shine.

Conclusion

*For the whole law can be summed up in this one
command: Love your neighbor as yourself.*
—Galatians 5:14 NLT

Now that you've read the book, where do you go from here?

It doesn't end when the last sentence has been read. That's just the beginning.

Like Alex, Tiana, Jamal, Bella, and Ethan, they realized it was the start of a journey, a challenge they accepted to get off their islands. Because, as you learned, no one is designed to be deserted and left alone. You were *made* to communicate. You were *made* to be with other people. It's a part of your life you have to get right if you want to realize your purpose and joy here on this earth, even if it scares the living daylights out of you. Building long-lasting relationships means you're going to have to step out and get your feet wet.

It doesn't matter if you're not a born talker or if you have the gift of gab. There's room to improve for every single one of us. Even if you can string words together faster than a cheetah chasing an antelope, you can still learn more about healthier conversations and better listening techniques.

It's why we began learning about listening and why it's the first thing we need to start with to become better in conversations. Everyone wants to be heard, not just you! So, give it a try, no matter whether you figured out if you're aggressive or passive in your communication style. Make it a priority to actively pay attention. You might be surrounded by friends, but if you don't listen properly, it's as good as being stranded in the middle of the sea! Using your bodies, minds, and words, you can become effective in the art of listening to what others have to say. Whether you speak a lot or hardly ever, you'll see others responding more to you just because you make the effort and take the time to pay attention.

So, start by opening your ears and your mind.

Then you can move on to thinking about the message you're trying to send. Not just by using words confidently but also by your body and facial expressions. You can learn ways to convey and express what's on your mind much more clearly. Remember that 90% of what you say is in the way you move and act. It makes sense to focus not just on the words you use, but also on how you handle yourself in the conversations. You need to be aware of the messages you're sending out by the way you sit or stand, how you look at others as you talk, and what you do with your hands. Your body language sometimes speaks louder than you do! The non-verbal signals won't just tell others if you're confident; they will also tell you!

And just as you saw, there are habits to learn. There are also behaviors you need to avoid or unlearn. Knowing which verbal and non-verbal cues can cause conversations to crash and burn will help even more. Those of you who are more like Tiana and Alex, reserved and quiet, can send the wrong message and shut down conversations even before they begin. And even if you're confident and outspoken like Bella and Ethan, your aggressive, dominating body language will do just as much harm. By steering clear of the roadblocks, you can achieve safer, more productive social interactions.

After putting these techniques of listening and talking into practice, you then learned about fine-tuning your social interactions. It's all great until you have nothing left to say or say the wrong things! Learning to start and carry on a casual conversation will genuinely give you confidence in any situation with anyone. You can begin making real connections without the fear of getting stuck on your own, staring at your feet with your mouth open and nothing coming out.

So, you've read the book and are trying these techniques to listen actively and speak more confidently. That's great. But remember, it's no good if you're alone in this. You might have days when the palm tree on your deserted island looks better than the world out there, and you think you don't want assistance. You might also think you're not afraid to say what's on your mind, so what's the big deal? You've got this without anyone's help.

But you're not meant to try to find your way off the deserted island you've been stranded on by swimming through shark-infested waters without any help. There are always people ready to give you a hand, share advice, and teach you new techniques. Others might know a little more than you and enthusiastically show you simpler, healthier ways to connect with others. Having your parents or guardians on board with you is like having a built-in lifeboat. They can make the difference between whether you sink, swim, get eaten alive, or rise up confidently and move forward successfully.

I have helped many teens through the stormy shark-infested waters they thought would pull them under using the tried-and-tested techniques in this book. I walked with them through their personal challenges, witnessing dramatic growth in communication and confidence. I counseled parents using these same strategies when they had issues with their teens. I must admit parents who practiced these strategies with their sons and daughters saw much faster growth followed by stronger bonds as they walked side by side through the challenges of the teen years.

Anyone, not just teenagers, can use most of what's in this book! I have seen parents' communication and social skills grow as they implemented these strategies with their teens. Relationships—healthy, mature, and deep—were formed because they all learned to speak appropriately and listen actively.

This book is a road map with signposts pointing toward healthy interactions and lasting relationships. It's a manual filled with instructions to help identify and fix bad habits to repair relationships. It's a journal of advice on what you can do to overcome personal social issues. It's also a guide on how to change situations with clever tips and tricks. It's a story. *Your story!*

As you've read through the book, use it as a map to help you to find your way in social situations. Think of each chapter as an instruction manual filled with the building blocks necessary to achieve better, closer, and more lasting relationships. Putting all these communication pieces together, you will begin to see the brighter picture—a better, more confident YOU. The person others seek to be with, desire to talk to, want to befriend, and even yearn to establish a lasting relationship in the journey forward.

Just like Alex and Tiana, who learned to step out and speak more, or Ethan and Bella, who had to learn to talk less, your story is being written. And the best part is it's not a complete story yet. There's still so much more to come, where the main characters see their dreams, discover love, and find themselves.

I've heard and seen many of these stories for myself, but I still get excited when someone tells me their own unique version of how they grew in confidence. I love hearing how people flourished because they saw how they could grow and change.

Having read through the book and adopted some of these techniques, I'm hoping you will also discover positive changes in your life. Maybe it happened quickly, or perhaps it took some time, with a few missteps along the way. If you're a teen or a parent, I want to hear YOUR story.

If this map, guide, or manual positively impacted you, then please share your appreciation by leaving a review of the book on Amazon. Let me know what you think, how it helped, and what worked. This will provide more insight for me to continue assisting others to form their stories better. One person's story can write another, and another, and another!

Enjoy living your story.

Enjoy feeling and being the CONFIDENT TEEN you were made to be!

Finally, brothers and sisters, whatever is true, whatever is noble, whatever is right, whatever is pure, whatever is lovely, whatever is admirable—if anything is excellent or praiseworthy—think about such things.
—Philippians 4:8 NIV

YOU COULD BE THE KEY TO SOMEONE ELSE'S TRANSFORMATION!

Now that you have all the tools you need to make your way toward a more confident and happy life, you're in an excellent position to help someone else.

Simply by leaving your honest opinion of this book on Amazon, you'll show other young people where they can find everything they need to improve their own confidence and happiness.

Thank you so much for your support. As we said, no one is designed to be left alone—and when we work together, we can make sure that no one is.

Appendix: Parenting Teenager Tips

When I was a boy of 14, my father was so ignorant I could hardly stand to have the old man around. But when I got to be 21, I was astonished at how much the old man had learned in seven years.
—Mark Twain

Sleepless nights during those first months after birth. The terrible twos. Toddler tantrums. First day of school. Getting called into school to deal with a situation. Even if we've read all the books, we're never really fully prepared for what actually happens to us as parents.

And then there are the teenage years!

Casual jokes and sweet remarks turn into disrespectful backtalk. Resentful looks reign supreme! Your bouncy child in the morning is replaced with someone who can't wake up anymore. Simple decisions become a crisis! They also seem to be easily distracted and constantly overwhelmed. They're going through body changes, emotional roller coasters, and understanding their role in this world. It's a period of adaptation and evolution. So, we also have to modify our approach to parenting.

Don't be afraid of sudden outbursts or sudden lengthy silences. These can be expected from time to time. By acknowledging who they are and where they're at, we can adjust our attitude and be the parent they deserve and desire.

If you've already read through the other chapters in this book, you're a step ahead. You may even see some of Alex, Tiana, Jamal, Bella, or Ethan in your own home. This will provide you with helpful insights into their world and their challenges. It will also show you meaningful techniques you and your teen can adopt to avoid arguments, reduce miscommunications and ease tense stand-offs.

In a study, 5,000 adults answered the question of what they wished their parents had done differently during moments of conflict, and three responses kept coming up:

1. They wished their parents had listened more.
2. They wished there had been more time to talk about feelings.
3. They wished they had spoken more to their parents.

(Smalley & Smalley, 2005)

Young children and teens learn from what they see more than what they hear. Parents are the example-setters. The way we communicate sets the blueprint for them to follow. If it's loud and chaotic, then that's what we're teaching and can expect in return. Emotionally distant parents often end up having emotionally distant teens (Vondruska, 2017). Aggressive behavior is learned and passed on, but so is healthy, balanced behavior and attitude in the home.

WHAT PARENTS CAN DO

Setting the tone in conversations can give our teens a head start on learning how to communicate appropriately. Here are a few tips and tricks to remember.

- **Understanding Teenage Development**

  "You just don't understand!"

That's a phrase we often hear as parents. Teens feel so misunderstood by society, friends, teachers, and us. By making the effort to try and understand what's happening with them physically, mentally, and emotionally, we can improve our ability to connect with them.

One of the reasons teenagers regularly challenge their parents is they're asking for more autonomy. They want to feel more in control because all the changes they experience can be overwhelming. Their desire for more independence can turn an insignificant topic into an uphill battle. The bombardment of emotions and physical changes can ramp up even small situations to crisis levels.

If we want to communicate with our teens properly, we need to understand where they are in their life right now. This gives us better insight into their behavior and more realistic expectations. It's like defusing a bomb! Instead of screaming at it or pushing it out of the way, we can take a breath and look at how it works. Then, we might see the one wire to clip, diffusing the issue before it explodes! Power struggles can also be disarmed and disabled to create a more pleasant environment at home for everyone involved.

- **Don't Label**

"You have more potential." "You're so lazy." "Your room is always a mess." "Stop being such a drama queen all the time!"

These are just a few of the more classic lines we may use. Even if they're true at the moment, by saying them out loud, our teens can feel like it's how we always see them. And one thing we all hate is being put in a box, especially one we don't want to be in! Unknowingly, we hand out labels, and sometimes they stick. Labels can be extremely damaging because it harms how they view themselves. Even if we do it jokingly, the message is no less critical or clear!

Teens can start living up to our labels. Rosemary Solomon, in her research, says the "stigma associated with the label [results] in isolation or rejection from society, lowered expectations, self-blame, or guilt, and emotional distress" (skylarstarnes, 2021). If they think we believe they're lazy, they will start seeing themselves as lazy. How we talk to teens is extremely important because it can influence how they view themselves. Remember, labels are only suitable for foods, not people.

Labels often happen when we position ourselves above our teens, when we launch into another long lecture (something they really hate!), or swoop into their room on another drill inspection. Discovering different approaches can bring better results than us stripping them down to the level of a label.

Remember to love them for who they are and not for what they're doing.

- **Be There**

Presence seems to be the most effortless activity, but it ends up being one of the hardest as a parent! We do and say things because we feel it's expected of us. Like everyone else, we're afraid of awkward silences. We feel better filling the silent voids with our wise advice, long lectures, stories of how we used to do things, and so on. But sometimes, it's best to let the silence be and not fill the space with words and just be there for our teens!

You don't always have to have an answer for everything!

Ethan's dad needed to learn to swallow his words and just be there for his son in these moments. Instead of allowing for silent space, he filled it with his thoughts, expanding until the bubble burst. After losing a game, Ethan just wanted to know his dad didn't look down on him for dropping a simple catch. All he longed for was a pat on the back. But instead, he got pointers on how he could have done better, why the mistake happened, and how he could have avoided letting his team down.

This healthy shift will allow your teen the open space they crave to share their feelings when they're ready. When your teen knows they can talk to you about anything and everything, their willingness to talk increases. Your open space paves the way for better conversations and healthier discussions. Instead of judging or responding, simply stop and listen. Try to understand where your teen is coming from instead of assuming you already know. The active listening skills discussed in previous chapters are helpful for both parents and teens. Modeling correct listening behavior sets the best example.

- **Recognize the Good**

Everyone likes a pat on the back. Sometimes we even do it for ourselves so that we can feel good. It doesn't matter if we're 4, 14, or 40; we all love to be acknowledged. Studies show we respond to social approval the same way we do when receiving a cash prize or reward (Bhanji & Delgado, 2013).

Sometimes we selectively only praise the good our teens do—a clean bedroom, a glowing report card, or performing well on the stage or sports field. But just focusing on results means we will miss out on the good being done in the process. Acknowledging the effort being made is just as important and encourages them to keep on trying.

For instance, if you see your child has been working harder on a subject, they were previously struggling in, praise their efforts. By doing this, you're setting them up for success. If you only focus on the end result, it increases their stress and can create resentment, causing them to withdraw. By encouraging them in the good work or effort they are doing, we create moments of bonding for parents and teens.

- **Make Quality Time**

Jamal's mom was always busy preparing dinner when she chose to try to catch up on how his day went, finding out about what happened in classes and how his studies were going. She was bustling around the kitchen while checking work messages at the same time, and he was glued to his phone. Questions were asked, answers were mumbled, and it looked like they were spending time together, but it wasn't quality. And meals in front of the TV were further distractions to both of them!

Where to find time to sit down and have a meaningful conversation? There just isn't enough time. That's why it's quality time because it's costly! Meaningful conversations don't happen while we are multitasking. Jamal was worried about a test the next day and tried to say something about it. His mom paused between checking her phone and putting dinner on the stove long enough to ask him to tell her. When she carried on, he just shrugged his shoulders and mumbled it wasn't such a big deal. Sooner or later, our teens will withdraw and stop reaching out to us because they see by our actions we're not really listening.

We need to consciously stop and plan quality time with our teens in our daily routine. Perhaps we can pause before they go to bed or turn off the TV during dinner. Even if we can only fit in 20 minutes, we need to do it to give them our undivided attention. Look at the chapter on good communication, where we emphasize the need to remove all distractions, so we can focus on what they're trying to say to us. Eliminating distractions and focusing our full attention on our teens sets a positive tone for our conversations. It shows them we value them and honestly want to listen to them.

• Understand Their Feelings

As we listen to our teen's words, it's essential to pay attention to the feelings behind their words. This is only possible by being an active listener. Remember, they're going through a lot of emotional changes. No matter how far-fetched the situation or feeling sounds, it's very real to them. By picking up on their emotional cues, it becomes easier to regulate our responses. If they're having a meltdown, there's no point in us losing our cool or shouting. This will only increase the waves rocking their boat, which is already struggling to stay afloat in their stormy sea.

We need to try to understand their feelings. We can encourage them to talk about their feelings by being open about ours. Our honest sharing creates a good example when teens see we are in touch with our emotions and don't let our feelings get the better of us. Our shared feelings are a significant step toward honest, deep conversation.

- **Talk Like Adults**

Teens want to be treated as adults, but they're just not there yet. It's a weird stage—not a child any longer, but not yet an adult! So, we need to help them with the transition, and one of the ways is to begin showing how adults talk, respond, and react. Treating them with respect, in the tone and language of an adult, will help them to start behaving more grown up.

We will find that the topics shift from childish ventures to more mature issues. Remember that teens' brains are wired to learn faster and try new things during adolescence, so we need to feed them (Alton, 2019).

The link between the two halves of a teenage brain matures, and so does the ability to think abstractly, reason things out, and make connections between ideas (Home-Start, 2020). Instead of just telling your teen to do something, followed by "because I said so" if there's resistance. Take a moment to address them as you would another adult. Explain the reason for your request and why they should do it when possible. These simple explanations model adult conversations and make them more receptive to your requests. They will be more understanding and follow through with little to no pushback.

- **Use "We"**

Building a relationship is a bit like forming a team. One of the ways to do this is by including everyone in the plans and discussions, and language is critical. By using "we" instead of "you" or "I," we develop team spirit. We are gathering everyone on the same side with a common purpose or task and allowing everyone to feel more empowered instead of being bossed around. This technique can help defuse any power bomb waiting to detonate the moment we ask them to do something.

Using "we" is not a trick to get things done but a strategy to assist in many situations. Deciding what to do on the weekend can be a family issue involving everyone. Trying to figure out what takeout to order can be a "we" matter. It can also be used in discussions where we can align with our teens on an issue. Fulfilling relationships are never "you or me" but always "we."

- **Have Patience**

How many times during a single day have any of us wanted to lose our cool and jump ship? We feel our teens just pushed us over the edge too many times. But reacting will only cause further damage, igniting the bomb already set to explode. Becoming aggressive causes them to behave defensively.

Having our hot buttons pushed is one area we will face over and over again during their teenage years. Staying patient with anyone is difficult. Taking a deep breath and staying calm is the only way to avoid nuclear war. We will need to practice and probably not get it right on a number of occasions, but when we do, the results will be worth it.

By staying cool in the face of chaos, we are not only setting a calming tone and good example, but we are consciously taking the hot air out of the balloon. If our emotions feel like they will betray us, we can ask for some time to have a break and return to the conversation when we feel calm again. It's an excellent technique to alleviate the tension and pressure while practicing adult emotion regulation.

We also need to avoid catastrophizing! When our teen drops a bombshell, it won't help if we freak out and react. They will quickly realize we can't handle their truth, and the door to those conversations will quickly slam closed.

• **Empathize**

Most teens feel as though they're the only ones facing something, even if millions of others have gone or are currently going through the exact same thing. They are learning to deal with a complex and chaotic world and sometimes struggle to cope with all its options. As a parent or guardian, we are responsible for showing compassion and empathy to guide our teens.

Keep your judgments out of the conversation. Try providing care and compassion. They want to be heard and understood. Ask questions to gain a better understanding and demonstrate that you genuinely want to know what they're going through. We can't belittle them by saying, "Oh, that's nothing. I once…" or "It doesn't seem so bad…" and other words diminishing their issue. From their youthful perspective, it is "that bad."

Be in the moment with them.

- **Ask Good Questions**

Remember the phrase "You just don't understand..."? There are ways we really can try to do just that—understand.

Ask questions. Not simple, one-word-answer questions, but open-ended, clarifying ones allowing them to explore their situation and giving you needed insight into their position to provide you a clearer picture. Not only will you gain some perspective on their issue, but you will also be demonstrating active listening. Just remember not to ask too many questions, or your conversation could quickly be seen as an interrogation drawing everything to a dead stop.

We might not understand their need for something like a new phone, concert tickets, sports gear, fancy clothes, or anything else we perceive as unnecessary. But there's no harm in asking about it rather than shutting down the subject. Perhaps they want to go somewhere. Instead of saying "No!" immediately, ask what it's about, why it's happening, or who's going. These reveal you are open to thinking about it before making an uninformed decision that could fuel resentment.

- **Give Validation**

Validation goes a very long way with teens. Everyone wants to know they have been actually heard and acknowledged. It's a potent tool in any conversation, even more so with our teens. One thing they crave is to be heard—honestly heard—by their parents.

Validation is not the same as agreeing with what has been said or done. Our words don't condone their words or actions. Instead, they establish that we have heard and seen them. If there's an emotional outburst, we can validate the emotions they're exhibiting. We can say, "I see you're frustrated and angry," "I understand you're not happy with..." or "Thanks for sharing with me. I can see you're stressed." These comments set the stage for a more positive conversation to follow. It's good to remember they might not know precisely how to express themselves adequately or even what emotion they want to show. By validating them, we don't shut them down but give room for further discussion and even a chance for them to express themselves more clearly.

> *When we regard teens with a positive, optimistic*
> *attitude, they give us their best.*
> —Lucie Hemmen

- **Don't Force**

When there's an issue or a problem, typically, we want to jump in, ready to save, solve, and sort it out. It's our job as parents, right? But there are times when we also need to step back and not say anything until the time comes to do so. Knowing when to start a conversation and when to end one are effective techniques.

Even though we can clearly see the issue, the potential solution means little to our teens as they might still be struggling to define the situation. They might not be prepared to talk about it. If we force the conversation, it's like breaking down the door instead of knocking, and teens are very guarded over their privacy! It can cause more damage than whatever has already taken place.

Stepping into a conversation is tricky. If we can't correctly read cues and body language indicating for us to continue or stop, there's nothing wrong with ending the conversation. The trick is to know when not to overdo it.

As a single parent, Bella's mom had to work hard to create a space where Bella could learn better communication. Even though her very outspoken daughter seemed confident, she was alienating friends and hurting her chances of building lasting relationships. It took mother and daughter a number of months to practice, talk, and figure out what worked and what didn't to see clear results at home and school. Finding the time to do it was not easy for a single parent carrying the load of a household alone; however, Bella's mom realized it wasn't a sacrifice she was making to help her daughter but an investment in Bella's life skills.

As parents, the job isn't over once the teenage years begin. Experts agree the first eight or so formative years are some of the most important to establish a child physically, socially, and mentally (Sacks, 2020). But through adolescence, parenting is no less crucial, and we can either inhibit or encourage this growth phase.

Teens may not want to admit it, but they still need their parents! Working from a solid base at home is the best platform to launch out into the world with a healthy, confident identity. One of the ways to do this is to ensure open and honest communication happens. It will provide a safe, secure environment in the face of a chaotic world and strengthen the bonds between them and us.

QUESTIONS TO ASK

Maybe like Tiana's parents, you want to make conversation, but the age gap means you're out of touch with their trends. Her parents' questions were met with a blank stare from Tiana as though they were speaking an alien dialect to an extraterrestrial on a foreign planet. They didn't know what to ask, and she didn't know how to respond—lost in translation!

There's nothing worse than a dad or mom trying hard to be with it and not pulling it off well! It can be cringe-worthy. Instead of trying to win your teen over to your world and interests, begin finding out about theirs. If you're clueless, don't panic. It just takes a bit of research to discover the trending social media, apps, movies, series, and fashions.

Here are a few conversation starters for you to try with your teen.

- If you could live anywhere, where would you choose?
- Do you still use TikTok and Instagram, or is there something new?
- What's the one thing that scares you the most?
- What's your opinion on (a specific current event)?
- What makes you truly happy?
- I see you haven't seen (name of a friend) lately. What's going on with them?
- If you could do anything you want for a day, what would you do?
- What would you do if you were the president?
- Do you sometimes feel lonely?
- Who's your favorite celebrity?
- What's your favorite song at the moment?
- When you're sad, what makes you feel better?
- What do you do when your friends ask you to do something you don't want to?
- What's one thing you remember from your childhood?
- What if you no longer had (something they enjoy)?
- What do you think I like most about you?

- What's your favorite subject at school?

(Perry, 2020)

OUTSIDE HELP

Alex is fortunate to have two supportive parents, ready to step in and do whatever will help their son. They just had no clue where to start or how to get past Alex's walls. Using some of these techniques, they both tried and saw slight progress. Soon, they realized the need for someone else's help. Where one part of the barricade came down, Alex would put up two more.

They needed a qualified, trusted person who could get through to Alex where they could not. They came to me seeking assistance.

Counseling doesn't mean you've lost the fight, thrown in the towel, or you're handing over your responsibility. It means you are making a conscious effort to go the extra mile. It means you will do what it takes to get to the breakthrough. Sometimes teens feel safer opening up a bit more to others than to their own parents, no matter how much we love them! It's no shame on a parent. We aren't all trained to deal with everything that comes our way.

And if the behavior patterns are outside the norm, then it's best to consult someone who deals with those issues and knows how to work with teens. Alex wasn't as severe a case as some of the other teens I've seen, but his parents made the right call, and after a few weeks of sessions where we spoke and ran through these techniques and exercises, we saw evident progress. Since then, Alex has learned to lower his walls. He still enjoys not being the center of attention, but he's very pleased with who he is, and his friends are thankful for the changes too. And best of all, there's no longer a barricade between him and his parents.

Ethan and his dad spent time with a local counselor from their church. It was someone they both trusted, and he was qualified in the field of conflict resolution. By being open about their issues and the need for help, both father and son could work through their behavioral habits and find better ways of solving arguments at home. They needed someone to help walk them through the minefields of their anger and harsh words. Seeing their relationship today is a testimony to how we can all benefit from help when needed.

Parenting is one of the greatest gifts anyone can have in their life, and like any true gift, it comes with its own set of challenges and rewards. Never give in to the temptation to throw in the towel. Instead, stay rooted in the joys surrounding parenting. You are a treasure to your family, and they are a gift given in love to you.

If you need assistance with your teen but are unsure who to trust or who's qualified, search for dependable helpers in your area that meet your requirements. Here are a few resources and suggestions in the United States:

American Psychological Association—Psychologist Locator: http://locator.apa.org/

American Association of Marriage and Family Therapy Locator: https://www.aamft.org/Directories/Find_a_Therapist.aspx

American Board of Professional Psychology Locator: https://abpp.org/Directory

American Academy of Child and Adolescent Psychiatry (AACAP): http://www.aacap.org/AACAP/Families_and_Youth/Resources/CAP_Finder.aspx

Association for Behavioral and Cognitive Therapies: https://www.findcbt.org/FAT/

Hospital and University Related ADHD Centers: http://www.chadd.org/Understanding-ADHD/About-ADHD/Professionals-Who-Diagnose-and-Treat-ADHD/Hospital-and-University-ADHD-Centers.aspx

Information on Mental Health Services and Resources: https://www.mentalhealth.gov/get-help

National Association of Social Workers: http://www.helpstartshere.org/?page_id=3677

SAHMSA's Behavioral Health Treatment Services Locator: https://findtreatment.samhsa.gov/

References

Alton, N. S. (2019, July 26). *Put on Your Hard Hat: Your Teen's Brain is Under Construction.* Your Teen Magazine. https://yourteen-mag.com/health/physical-health/teenage-brain-development

Anon. (2009, October 22). *How to Read Body Language.* Teen Ink. https://www.teenink.com/opinion/love_relationships/article/141786/How-to-Read-Body-Language/

Arcand, J. (2020, January 30). *12 Fascinating Quotes About Work-Life Balance.* Work It Daily. https://www.workitdaily.com/quotes-about-work-life-balance/

AT&T. (1995). *Active Listening Self-Assessment Are You an Active Listener?* Executive Excellence. https://executiveexcellence.com/wp-content/uploads/2019/05/ActiveListening-SelfAssessment_Fillable.pdf

Barker, K. L. (2008). *NIV Study Bible: New International Version.* Zondervan.

Bhanji, J. P., & Delgado, M. R. (2013). The Social Brain and Reward: Social Information Processing in the Human Striatum. *Wiley Interdisciplinary Reviews: Cognitive Science, 5(1),* 61–73. https://doi.org/10.1002/wcs.1266

Bhaskar, S. (2022, March 8). *How to Have Effective Communication With Your Teen.* ChildrensMD. https://childrensmd.org/browse-by-age-group/teens/how-to-have-effective-communication-with-your-teen/

Boone, A. (2022). *5 Reasons to Smile While Speaking*. Ethos3.com. https://ethos3.com/5-reasons-to-smile-while-speaking/

Brabham, M. (2022, July 28). *The Art of Friendship: How to Start Conversations That Attract Friends*. Shondaland. https://www.shondaland.com/live/family/a40731772/the-art-of-friendship-how-to-start-conversations/

Caballero, I. K. (2018, September 1). *The Importance of Communication in Today's Digital World*. Www.linkedin.com. https://www.linkedin.com/pulse/50-amazing-ways-inspire-you-communicate-more-todays-world-caballero/

Catholic Bible Press. (2021). *NRSVCE, Illustrated Catholic Bible*. Zondervan.

Chein, J., Albert, D., O'Brien, L., Uckert, K., & Steinberg, L. (2011). Peers Increase Adolescent Risk Taking by Enhancing Activity in the Brain's Reward Circuitry. *Developmental Science, 14(2),* *F1–F10*. https://doi.org/10.1111/j.1467-7687.2010.01035.x

The Common Roadblocks to Healthy Communication. (2022, March 10). Achology. https://achology.com/the-common-roadblocks-to-healthy-communication/

Communication Checks: A Self-Quiz. (n.d.). University of Washington. https://depts.washington.edu/uwhatc/PDF

Davis, M. (2015). *Hormones and the Adolescent Brain*. Brain Facts. https://www.brainfacts.org/thinking-sensing-and-behaving/childhood-and-adolescence/2015/hormones-and-the-adolescent-brain-120915

Economy, Peter. (2015, November 5). *26 Brilliant Quotes on the Super Power of Words*. Inc Africa. https://incafrica.com/library/peter-economy-26-brilliant-quotes-on-the-super-power-of-words

Eliot, T. S. (n.d.). *Four Quartets*. Philoctetes. http://philoctetes.org/documents/Eliot Poems.pdf

English Standard Version Bible. (2001). Crossway Bibles.

Heltler, S. (2015, July 6). *How Good Are You at the Art of Conversation? A Quiz*. Psychology Today. https://www.psychologytoday.com/za/blog/resolution-not-conflict/201507/how-good-are-you-the-art-conversation-quiz

Holland, K. (2018, June 4). *Phubbing: What Is It, Effects on Relationships, and How to Stop*. Healthline. https://www.healthline.com/health/phubbing

Holt-Lunstad, J., Smith, T. B., Baker, M., Harris, T., & Stephenson, D. (2015, March 1). *Loneliness and Social Isolation as Risk Factors for Mortality: A Meta-Analytic Review*. Perspectives on Psychological Science: A Journal of the Association for Psychological Science. https://pubmed.ncbi.nlm.nih.gov/25910392/

Holy Bible, KJV. (2014). Thomas Nelson Pub.

The Holy Bible: NKJV New King James Version. (2016). Holman Bible Publishers.

How Much of Communication Is Nonverbal? (2020, November 3). University of Texas Permian Basin. https://online.utpb.edu/about-us/articles/communication/how-much-of-communication-is-nonverbal/

How to Keep a Conversation Going. (2020, June 17). The Cut. https://www.thecut.com/article/how-to-keep-a-conversation-going.html

How to Understand and Read Body Language. (2021, October 21). Psych Central. https://psychcentral.com/health/body-language

Ives, C. (2022). *50 Funny Questions to Start a Conversation.* Signup Genius. https://www.signupgenius.com/groups/funny-questions-for-conversation.cfm

Klipsch-Abudu, K. (2020, February 5). *Healthy Communication for Teens: Everything You Need to Know.* Mount Sinai Adolescent Health Center. https://www.teenhealthcare.org/blog/healthy-communication-teens/

Kramer, B. (2019, May 21). *Council Post: Why It's Time to Stop Labeling Ourselves and Those Around Us.* Forbes. https://www.forbes.com/sites/forbescoachescouncil/2019/05/21/why-its-time-to-stop-labeling-ourselves-and-those-around-us/?sh=a8a0dd0433dd

Loneliness and the Workplace. (2020). https://www.cigna.com/static/www-cigna-com/docs/about-us/newsroom/studies-and-reports/combatting-loneliness/cigna-2020-loneliness-factsheet.pdf

Miller, K. (2021, November 18). *12 Tips for How to End a Conversation, Sans Awkwardness.* Well and Good. https://www.wellandgood.com/how-to-end-conversation/

NLT Study Bible. (2008). Tyndale House Pub.

O., Bri. (2017, April 11). *Do You Talk Too Much?* Zoo. https://www.zoo.com/quiz/do-you-talk-too-much-zoo

References

Perry, C. (2020, May 28). *Ask Your Teen These 20 Questions and You Could Come Out of the Convo Closer.* Parents. https://www.parents.com/kids/teens/questions-for-teens-to-help-you-bond/

Pulsifier, C. (2020). *Inspirational Words of Wisdom For You.* Wow 4 U. https://www.wow4u.com

Pulsifer, C., & Gillison, B. (n.d.). *57 quotes about helping others. Inspirational Words of Wisdom. https://www.wow4u.com/helping/*

Quick Quiz: How Well Do You Know the Teen Brain? (2008, November 26). USNews. https://health.usnews.com/health-news/family-health/brain-and-behavior/articles/2008/11/26/quick-quiz-how-well-do-you-know-the-teen-brain

Quotes-tagged Speaker. (2022). Quotesperation. https://quotesperation.com/Quotes/Tag/speaker?p=3&s=9

Rutsch, E. (n.d.). *Culture of Empathy Builder: Rachel Naomi Remen.* Culture of Empathy. http://cultureofempathy.com/References/Experts/Others/Rachel-Naomi-Remen.htm

Sacks, P. (2020, December 15). *The Formative Years & Erik H. Erikson's Eight Stages of Development.* https://www.paulasacks.com/formative-years/

Sheely, G. (2014, April 2). *When Praise Backfires.* 1eighty Consulting. https://1eightyconsulting.com/when-praise-backfires/

Simao, K. (2020, October 25). *10 Celebrities Who Were Shy In High School.* TheThings. https://www.thethings.com/celebrities-shy-in-high-school/

Smalley, G., & Smalley, G. (2005). *The DNA of Parent-Teen Relationships.* Tyndale House Publishers.

Soken-Huberty, E. (2021, March 26). *10 Reasons Why Listening Is Important*. The Important Site. https://theimportantsite.com/1 0-reasons-why-listening-is-important/

Starnes, Skylar. (2021, July 13). *The Power of Labels*. Turner Syndrome Foundation. https://turnersyndromefoundation.org/2021/07/13/ the-power-of-labels/

Teens and Mobile Phones. (2010, April 20). Pew Research Center. https://www.pewresearch.org/internet/2010/04/20/teens-and-mobile-phones-3/

Templeton, J. (2017, November 6). *The 8 Pillars of Holistic Health and Wellness*. Ask the Scientists. https://askthescientists.com/pillars -of-wellness/

Tozer, C. (2016, September 27). *Social & Emotional Changes in Adolescence*. Bridging the Gap. https://www.btg.org.au/socia l-emotional-changes-in-adolescence

A Treasury of Ageless, Sovereign Grace, Devotional Writings. (n.d.). Grace Gems. https://www.gracegems.org/

Types of Listening. (2011). Skills You Need. https://www.skill-syouneed.com/ips/listening-types.html

Understanding the Teenage Brain. (2020, May 18). Home-Start Central Bedfordshire. https://www.home-startcentralbeds.org. uk/understanding-the-teenage-brain/

Van Dijk, S. (2012). *DBT Made Simple: A Step-by-Step Guide to Dialectical Behavior Therapy*. New Harbinger Publications.

References

Van Edwards, V. (2021, January 19). *16 Essential Body Language Examples and Their Meanings*. Science of People. https://www.scienceof people.com/body-language-examples/

Vondruska, B. (2017, July 25). *What Parents' Examples Mean to Children*. The Kind of Parent You Are. https://www.thekindofparen tyouare.com/articles/what-parents-examples-mean-to-children

Warner, M. (2021, April 30). *Communication Styles—The Mouse, the Lion, the Fox, and the Owl*. UTHealth Houston McGovern Medical School Louis A. Faillace, MD, Department of Psychiatry and Behavioral Sciences. https://med.uth.edu/ psychiatry/2021/04/30/communication-styles-the-mous e-the-lion-the-fox-and-the-owl/

Webster, Noah. (2021, September 29). *Your Child's Brain on Digital Cocaine: With Brad Huddleston*. Noah Webster Educational Foundation. https://noahwebstereducationalfoundation.org/you r-childs-brain-on-digital-cocaine-with-brad-huddleston/

Woods, J. J. (2022). *Survival Debate (Rewind): Team Up or Go It Alone*. Survival Cache. https://survivalcache.com/survival-debat e-group-survival-solo-survival/

Zipkin, N. (2014, July 17). *Richard Branson: Strong Leaders Are Good Listeners*. Entrepreneur. https://www.entrepreneur.com/leadership/ richard-branson-strong-leaders-are-good-listeners/235540

Made in the USA
Las Vegas, NV
03 December 2024

13339672R10089